Effective Crisis Leadership in Healthcare

Lessons Learned from a Pandemic

Aimee Greeter, MPH, FACHE

Max Reiboldt, CPA

COKER GROUP

Copyright © 2021 by American Association for Physician Leadership®

978-0-9848311-7-3 Print
978-0-9848311-8-0 eBook
Published by **American Association for Physician Leadership, Inc.**
PO Box 96503 | BMB 97493 | Washington, DC 20090-6503

Website: www.physicianleaders.org

AAPL books are available at special quantity discounts to use as premiums and sales promotions, or for use in corporate training programs. For more information, please write to Special Sales at journal@physicianleaders.org

This publication is designed to provide general information and is sold with the understanding that neither the author nor the publisher is engaged in rendering legal, accounting, ethical, or clinical advice. If legal or other expert advice is required, the services of a competent professional person should be sought.

13   8 7 6 5 4 3 2 1

Copyedited, typeset, indexed, and printed in the United States of America

PUBLISHER
Nancy Collins

EDITORIAL ASSISTANT
Jennifer Weiss

DESIGN & LAYOUT
Carter Publishing Studio

COPYEDITOR
Patricia George

Table of Contents

Acknowledgments

The information in this book represents many Coker Group contributors' perspectives based on their years of working with clients in the healthcare industry. We value their knowledge and abilities.

We continue to enjoy working with Nancy Collins, publisher, and Jennifer Weiss, editorial assistant. We value the confidence they express in the knowledge that Coker Group maintains. Thank you for an enduring and satisfying professional relationship.

Kay B. Stanley, FACMPE, Editor

About the Authors

Aimee Greeter, MPH, FACHE, is a senior vice president at Coker Group with specialized ability in business strategy, mergers and acquisitions, transaction advisory, physician alignment, accountable care responsiveness, hospital service line development, clinical integration initiatives, strategic plan development, executive compensation, employee compensation, crisis communications, operational efficiency, and financial management.

Aimee works with nonprofit and for-profit hospitals and health systems of all sizes and larger single- and multi-specialty physician practices to achieve their strategic and tactical goals. Additionally, she manages the firm's delivery of alignment and transaction services. The team works with some of the largest and most prestigious health systems in the U.S. on their business initiatives, as well as with independent community hospitals, academic medical centers, ambulatory surgery centers, critical access hospitals, outpatient facilities, and medical practices in all 50 states. Specifically, Aimee and her colleagues spend time with healthcare organizations in the provider space on their buyside acquisitions, divestiture of assets, strategic partnerships, and transactions.

Aimee is a popular speaker and often is engaged by highly respected organizations across the nation to speak to health systems, medical groups, legal associations, and other healthcare constituents. She has authored many articles and books on topics such as hospital–physician alignment, clinician engagement, practice mergers, professional service agreements (PSAs), and executive leadership. Contact Aimee at agreeter@cokergroup.com.

Max Reiboldt, CPA, is the president/CEO of Coker Group. He has experienced first-hand the ongoing changes of healthcare providers, which uniquely equips him to handle strategic, tactical, financial, and management issues that health systems and physicians face in today's evolving marketplace.

Max understands the nuances of the healthcare industry, especially in such a dynamic age. He understands how healthcare organizations need to maintain viability in a highly competitive market. His position of having "experienced everything" in the healthcare industry equips him to supply pertinent counsel to clients. Whether a transitional provider or a more trailblazing healthcare entity, he is uniquely qualified to work with these organizations to provide sound solutions to every day and long-range challenges.

As president/CEO, Max oversees Coker Group's services and its general operations. He has a passion for working with clients and organizations of all sizes and engages in consulting projects nationwide.

A graduate of Harding University, he is a licensed certified public accountant in Georgia and Louisiana, and a member of the American Institute of Certified Public Accountants, Georgia Society of CPAs, Healthcare Financial Management Association, and American Society of Appraisers. He is also a member of the American College of Healthcare Executives. Contact Max at mreiboldt@cokergroup.com.

Mark Reiboldt, MA, is senior vice president and director of strategy at Coker Group, where he specializes in financial and transaction advisory for hospitals, medical groups, and other healthcare organizations. These transactions include mergers and acquisitions, divestitures, equity purchases, physician alignment deals, and joint ventures.

Mark's advisory services often entail acquisition/investment due diligence, valuation services, transaction management, buyside representation, strategic alternatives processes, and post-merger integration.

As director of strategy, he serves on the executive leadership team and works with the firm's senior management on strategic projects. He is a board member and secretary of the Coker Foundation, the firm's nonprofit charity organization. Contact Mark at markreiboldt@cokergroup.com.

Roz Cordini, JD, MSN, RN, CHC, CHPC, is a senior vice president and director of coding and compliance services with Coker Group. Roz leads the coding and compliance service line to focus on Office of Inspector General program compliance, including compliance program development, compliance effectiveness reviews, compliance investigations, physician compensation governance procedures, and governance education.

She delivers advisory services to boards of directors and senior leaders about compliance, virtual compliance officer services, provider documentation and coding audits, and other compliance-related services. These include physician arrangements audits, facilitation of root cause analyses/failure mode effectiveness, criticality analyses for identified compliance violations, and mergers and acquisitions compliance due diligence.

Coker Group's compliance services also include Health Insurance Portability and Accountability Act (HIPAA) privacy assessments and security risk analyses. Contact Roz at rcordini@cokergroup.com.

Taylor Cowart, MBA, is a senior associate with Coker Group's financial and hospital operations services division. She works predominantly in the financial and alignment services section, providing clients with consultative assistance for alignment and integration, financial analyses, compensation design, and service line development.

Taylor also works with accountable care-era response and preparation, helping clients respond to value-based reimbursement changes and developing population health management strategies. Her extensive experience in healthcare consulting includes the hospital administration arena, particularly in credentialing and privileging management. Contact Taylor at tcowart@cokergroup.com.

Jeffery Daigrepont, CAP, senior vice president at Coker Group, specializes in healthcare automation, system integration, cybersecurity, operations, and deployment of enterprise information systems for large integrated delivery networks and medical practices. His specific interests include data migration, vendor contracting, strategic IT planning and optimization, security, and compliance. Contact Jeffery at jdaigrepont@cokergroup.com.

Brandt Jewell, BBA, is a senior vice president at Coker Group where he leads the physician services team, which focuses on delivering value across all areas of ambulatory operations. He has extensive consulting experience related to executive leadership development, practice acquisitions, physician alignment strategies, operational efficiency, financial stability, organizational structures, revenue cycle management, and competitive landscapes for health systems and provider groups across the country.

Brandt partners with health systems, investors, and medical groups to implement operational solutions and strategies that improve provider entities' financial health. He also develops value-based care strategies for integrated networks of employed and independent providers. Contact Brandt at bjewell@cokergroup.com.

Alex Kirkland, MBA, is a vice president at Coker Group. He has more than 10 years of healthcare experience from a financial and operational background with an emphasis on physician compensation, reimbursement models, and population health. With Coker, he focuses primarily on physician alignment transactions, compensation trends, and payer reimbursement strategies. Contact Alex at akirkland@cokergroup.com.

Lee Perrett, BS, BA, a veteran recruiting executive and vice president at Coker Group, has more than 25 years of experience recruiting and placing senior-level executives and middle-management candidates within multiple disciplines and industries. These include hospitals, healthcare systems, medical group practices, consumer products, finance, consulting, and professional services. His experience is in partnering with client organizations in their leadership selection efforts for positions ranging from director to president/CEO.

Lee tailors every search assignment specifically for each job function and client and designs them to meet the unique requirements and strategic challenges for that role. A good fit with the organization's culture is a top priority. Contact Lee at lperrett@cokergroup.com.

About Coker Group

Coker Group, founded in 1987, has experienced continual growth for its 30-year history, with a reputation for being one of the most respected healthcare consulting firms. Their central office is in metropolitan Atlanta, Georgia, with additional offices in Charlotte, North Carolina, and Nashville, Tennessee, and consultants based throughout the United States.

Coker continues to be a trusted adviser to prominent healthcare organizations on a broad range of issues. Knowing that healthcare organizations are currently struggling to do more with less, Coker works with clients to develop customized solutions in five main service areas: finance, strategy and operations, human capital, technology, and compliance.

Coker focuses exclusively on healthcare, unlike many consulting firms that diversify into other areas. Their management team is competent in strategic planning and business development, healthcare mergers and acquisitions, healthcare financial pro formas, hospital management, operations, and technology. This ability extends to involvement in physician/provider and executive compensation assignments. Coker is considered an industry leader in the healthcare arena. Coker personnel have completed hundreds of feasibility projects, authored many books and white papers, and spoken at several national and regional conferences.

Coker's philosophy in delivering consultative assistance is to provide hospitals, physician practices, and other healthcare companies with innovative, principled solutions in strategic planning, business operations, finance, and information technology to achieve their optimum performance, financial return, and productivity.

Preface

Few of us have experienced a crisis as unsettling to all and devastating to millions as the COVID-19 pandemic. Clearly, emergencies come in many shapes and forms beyond tornadoes, hurricanes, floods, volcanic eruptions, and tsunamis. They bring loss of human life, pain, and suffering to all those directly affected by the crisis as well as their friends and loved ones. Some costs of crises can never be recovered.

As one of the most vital industries in the world, healthcare is obligated to always be operational in the face of whatever emergency arises. *Leadership in Crisis* presents strategies for preparing for a crisis, especially for those who deliver healthcare services. The guidance, based on substantial research, will help healthcare professionals apply many hard-learned lessons from the COVID-19 pandemic.

No one can predict the next widespread illness, weather emergency, or environmental incident. In the crucial business of delivering healthcare, we must expect the unexpected! It is never too early to plan for the future.

CHAPTER 1

What Is a "Crisis?"

The word "crisis" has a negative connotation that often evokes feelings of panic, anxiousness, fear, unrest, or agitation. Many crises arise unexpectedly, test previously unproven boundaries or capabilities, and are of a sufficient magnitude to make those directly and indirectly affected feel overwhelmed. However, a crisis also can spark new ideas, hone leaders' skills, and cause overlooked or underprioritized improvements and efficiencies in calmer waters. Thus, while a crisis may initially evoke panic, it may also yield benefits.

Crises can be prompted by natural disasters, civil disturbances, legal and regulatory challenges, environmental disruptions, and other challenges that individuals and organizations may encounter. In this chapter, we describe the characteristics of a crisis and address the gap in the social safety net that results from a crisis. We define what a crisis is and is not, categorize the types of crises, outline the human response to a crisis, and lay a foundation for more specific discussions to follow.

DEFINITION OF CRISIS

One definition of crisis, according to Merriam-Webster, is[1]:
  a. An unstable or crucial time or state-of-affairs in which a decisive change is impending, especially, one with the distinct possibility of a highly undesirable outcome.
  b. A situation that has reached a critical phase.

No matter what type of crisis is in play (and, as we note below, a crisis can take on many different forms), it often falls to leaders to make decisive changes during unstable times. Given that healthcare is a people-centered and people-driven industry, the outcome may affect the lives of many, thus amplifying the potential overall impact, whether either desirable or undesirable.

Crises in the healthcare space can be disruptive. Adequate education of leaders, preparation by the organization, and communication to stakeholders are critical to ensuring the impacts of a crisis are as positive as possible and, when negative, are short-lived.

Characteristics of Crises

Bundy *et al.*, identify the four primary characteristics of crises[2]:
1. Sources of *uncertainty, disruption, and change.*
2. *Harmful or threatening* for organizations and their stakeholders.
3. Behavioral phenomena, meaning they are socially constructed by those involved.
4. Parts of extensive *processes* rather than discrete events.

These characteristics apply to all types of crises (categorized below) and highlight the interrelatedness of crises and people. Every crisis likely will have a people element. That is, people either will be the cause of or will be affected by the crisis. This characteristic is important as it underscores the need to engage in pre-planning, mitigation, and post-crisis events. If people are central to a crisis (either as a cause or in its effects), they likewise are central to its mitigation and cessation.

Types of Crises

While crises can manifest in myriad ways, we can organize them into several overarching categories, as illustrated in Figure 1.1.[3]

Given that crises fall across a spectrum from minor to devastating, many organizations will deal with one at some time during their existence. Therefore, it is important not only to be aware of the many types of crises, but also to begin developing plans to address them when they arise.

Elements of a Crisis

The work of Keown-McMullan[4] identifies three primary elements of a crisis:
1. Triggering event
2. Perceived inability to cope
3. Threat to survival

Triggering Event

Although a crisis may build over time, one event often acts as a trigger that alerts people to the issue at hand. For example, while patient care

FIGURE 1.1. Types of Crises

Natural Crisis • Results from disruptions in nature and the environment. • Is outside the control of humans; often not directly man-made. • May include the following subcategories: —Geophysical (earthquakes, landslides, tsunamis, and volcanic activity) —Hydrological (avalanches and floods) —Climatological (extreme temperatures, drought, and wildfires) —Meteorological (cyclones, storms, wave surges)
Biological Crisis • Includes disease epidemics and plagues. • Has arisen in recent years as the seasonal influenza outbreak, the 2003 SARS epidemic, the 2015 Zika virus, and, most recently, the 2020 COVID-19 pandemic.
Technological Crisis • Results from a gap, failure, temporary, or permanent disruption in technology. • Encompasses technology equipment failures, malware and other corruptive software, and issues with system upgrades or replacements. • Is a more significant issue today due to destructive practices such as phishing attacks and ransomware.
Confrontation Crisis • Arises from individuals fighting among themselves. These conflicts can lead to strikes, boycotts, picketing, and other actions that may be temporary or last for an extended period and must be considered from both an internal perspective and in relation to the broader external environment, such as civil unrest based on racial, religious, or political affiliations. • Includes employee-to-supervisor conflict in which employees become insubordinate and disruptive. • Often results from a breakdown in communication and/or coordination.
Crisis of Malevolence • One of the most extreme forms of a crisis, is based on aggression and often premeditation. This includes criminal activity, such as kidnapping high-ranking executives.

(figure continues)

has always been the focal point within the healthcare industry, it was only when the Institute of Medicine (IOM) released its "Crossing the Chasm"[5] report in 2001 that people took notice of the massive gaps between best practices in the delivery of healthcare and the actual care patients received. The report opened many eyes to the fact that the findings from "To Err is Human"[6] were not merely fleeting issues but indicative of the need for a wholesale change in how providers interact

FIGURE 1.1. Types of Crises *(continued)*

Crisis of Organizational Misdeeds
• Arises when management makes decisions knowing there will be harmful consequences for key stakeholders and external parties. Manifests when superiors ignore the possible after-effects of strategies and implement them for quick results.
• Can be further classified into the following three types:
  1. Crisis of Skewed Management Values: Arises when management supports short-term growth and ignores broader issues.
  2. Crisis of Deception: Arises when management purposely tampers with data and information and makes disingenuous promises to customers.
  3. Crisis of Management Misconduct: Results when management deliberately indulges in illegal acts such as bribery, sharing confidential information, etc.

Crisis Based on Violence • Includes workplace violence, such as patients attacking nurses or employees attacking their colleagues or supervisors. • Includes terrorist attacks and other vicious behaviors.
Reputational Crisis • Includes rumors spread by disgruntled employees, negative posts on social media, inflammatory media coverage, poor Internet reviews, or the accurate sharing of significant clinical errors such as wrong-site surgery or suboptimal patient outcomes.
Legal or Regulatory Crisis • Within a highly regulated industry such as healthcare, can result when organizations run afoul of legal and regulatory structures, such as those within the Anti-Kickback Statute or the Physician Self-Referral Law (the Stark Law). • Can also result in reputational and financial crisis; may start as one type and develop over time to include other crisis forms.
Financial Crisis • Arises when an organization's financial standing is impacted, which can result from degradation of revenue, excessive expenses, or the lack of a profit margin. • May include bankruptcy proceedings to close or reorganize a business when the organization fails to pay its creditors or other interested parties. Bankruptcy proceedings can limit an organization's ability to access funds both for business and investment purposes and leading to a reputational crisis (see above).

Adapted from Management Study Guide: https://www.managementstudyguide.com/types-of-crisis.htm.

with and treat patients. In the aftermath of this second IOM report, the collective industry seemed to take stock and realize that every one of the six dimensions the IOM studied needed improvement.

Interestingly, while this type of "slow burn" leading to a crisis is possible (and was caused by decades of suboptimal care delivery), it is equally possible for a crisis to arise seemingly overnight. Natural crises are particularly disposed to this type of upheaval, coming on fast and requiring immediate attention. Regardless the circumstances, a trigger is necessary for a crisis to arise.

Perceived Inability to Cope

Once the event is triggered, it must be acknowledged; the subsequent reaction can turn it into a crisis. For example, leaders may perceive (correctly or incorrectly) that they cannot manage the change they are now confronting. They may believe the change is out of their control, that they are ill-equipped to deal with it, or that they do not have the resources or time to mitigate its effects. These perceptions contribute to the development of a crisis.

On the other hand, the leaders may feel confident in their ability to manage the change, leading to a different outcome. This highlights why the same event could occur in two organizations and result in a crisis in only one of them. As we emphasize throughout this book, leaders' abilities or capacities have a significant effect on the outcome of a crisis within an organization.

Threat to Survival

The third element of a crisis is a threat to the stability of an organization. The belief that significant change is necessary, combined with a perception that the organization's leaders are not equipped to manage the change, can put the organization's survival in jeopardy. When this third condition is met, a crisis arises.

In sum, the triggering event causes a significant change or has the potential to cause a significant change. The prompt alone is important, but the real impact comes when people notice it. When that happens, the leaders either believe they cannot effectively manage the change or are unwilling to address it, yielding the second contributing element to a crisis. Finally, when a trigger and the corresponding reaction are significant enough to cause or require change, the result can be a feeling of organizational instability or unsustainability. When these threats to the existence of the organization are significant enough, the conditions are ripe for a crisis.

The Basis of Behavioral Change

In 1943, Abraham Maslow proposed a psychological construct that identified a hierarchy of needs (see Figure 1.2).[7] Maslow's theory indicates that a person's lower-ranking needs (i.e., physiological needs such as food, water, clothing, warmth, and rest) must be met before they can attend to their higher-ranking needs (i.e., self-actualization needs, such as achieving one's full potential).

FIGURE 1.2. Maslow's Hierarchy of Needs

Source: Abraham Maslow, A Theory of Human Motivation, *1943.*

Crises can cause people to feel concerned, worried, and distressed because crises often threaten a person's lower-tier needs, thereby preventing that person from concentrating on higher-level needs and opportunities.

For example, Hurricane Harvey's landfall in Houston in August 2017 left many people stranded in their homes, concerned about their ability to access critical supplies, or even leave their homes for physically safer areas. In such situations, behavioral change is a near certainty, as people adjust their behaviors to accommodate their most pressing needs. This is important to note, as our expectations of people amid a crisis may need to be different from those during standard operations.

Responding Effectively to Behavioral Changes

The Centers for Disease Control and Prevention's Crisis & Emergency Risk Communication (CERC) center provides tools and resources to help leaders effectively communicate during an emergency. The CERC "Psychology of a Crisis" manual[8] an explanation is provided regarding the four ways people process information during a crisis. Along with explaining each, as in Figure 1.3, the manual also shares the key actions that should be considered in responding to a crisis.

FIGURE 1.3. Four Ways We Process Information During a Crisis

1. We simplify messages.

2. We hold on to current beliefs.

3. We look for additional information and opinions.

4. We believe the first message.

Source: CERC, "Psychology of a Crisis" 2019 Manual

For each of the four ways people are known to process information during a crisis, the CDC provides an actionable and effective response. We recommend the responses in Figure 1.4.

Recognizing how people's behavior changes throughout a crisis is an important part of the pre-planning processes and highlight the need for well-established and well-communicated crisis management plans. When people are in a situation where they cannot process their higher-order thinking, it is integral that plans have already been made that they can then merely execute.

Gaps in the Social Safety Net

One of the most eye-opening elements of crises is the exposure of gaps in the social safety net that exists within developed society to protect its citizens. In the case of a crisis in the healthcare environment, these gaps can be seen in the inability to access necessary care (e.g., rural areas without access to a critical specialty) or the inability to be seen based on ability to pay (e.g., some practices limit or disallow patients who are under- or over insured). These gaps are often

FIGURE 1.4. Responding Effectively to Behavioral Changes

Use Simple Messages	With too much information to comprehend, people tend to either tune out, listen to only pieces of the information (instead of hearing all the important details), or misinterpret what is said. Therefore, many organizations use acronyms when conveying critical information. For example, the American Stroke Association uses the F.A.S.T. description (Facial drooping, Arm weakness, Speech difficulties, and Time) to share the warning signs of stroke and what actions need to be taken. These actions are easily understood, simple messages that take little effort to remember.
Use Credible Sources for Messages.	When confronted with a crisis, many people revert to what they know, regardless of its accuracy at that moment. Thus, some will need to be convinced of an alternate truth to act. This highlights the need for trusted sources to share information on what is happening during a crisis and what actions are necessary.
Use consistent messages.	In our digital age and with widespread social media adoption in which additional information is seemingly always available, people will often continue to seek further information during a crisis. As a result, it is essential to use consistent messaging so there is no misinterpretation of varied messages. People must receive a confirmation on the correct path of action, which is for many a prerequisite to taking any action at all.
Release accurate messages as soon as possible.	How often have we seen friends, neighbors, or colleagues share information that they believe to be credible, and yet are their perception of the truth, as opposed to the truth itself? When a vacuum of information exists, people often create a flawed message to fill this void. Therefore, it is important that during a crisis, accurate information be shared as quickly as possible. Even if the information changes over time (as often occurs), it is important to begin communicating based on the then-current realities to allow people to understand better, lest they begin to create (or share) their own narrative.

Source: https://emergency.cdc.gov/cerc/ppt/CERC_Psychology_of_a_Crisis.pdf.

only surfaced in times of crisis, which make them difficult, and yet not impossible, to plan and account for during times when changes could more readily be made.

SUMMARY

While there are many types of crises, the reality is that they all test the capabilities of people and organizations. Within healthcare, crises can be a catalyst for disastrous outcomes, or they can be a catalyst for positive change. This outcome is dependent on how organizations organize themselves before, during, and after the crisis, and how effectively leadership can steward people throughout the events. In subsequent chapters, we provide effective methods on how to organize and how to lead to ensure your organization views crises as a catalyst for positive outcomes.

RESOURCES

1. Merriam-Webster. "Crisis." Merriam-Webster.com. www.merriam-webster.com/dictionary/crisis. Accessed March 2, 2021.
2. Bundy J, Pfarrer MD, Short, CE, et al. Crises and Crisis Management: Integration, Interpretation, and Research Development. *Journal of Management.* 43(6):1661-1692. https://doi.org/10.1177/0149206316680030. Accessed March 2, 2021.
3. Prachi J. Types of Crisis. Management Study Guide. Managementstudyguide.com. Accessed April 16, 2021.
4. Keown-McMullan C. Crisis: When Does a Molehill Become a Mountain? *Disaster Prevention and Management.* 6(1):1, 4-10. doi: 10.1108/09653569710162406.
5. Institute of Medicine. *Crossing the Quality Chasm: A New Health System for the 21st Century.* Washington, DC: National Academy Press, 2001.
6. Kohn LT, Corrigan J, & Donaldson MS. *To Err Is Human: Building a Safer Health System.* Washington, DC: National Academy Press, 2000.
7. Maslow AH. A Theory of Human Motivation. *Psychological Review.* 50(4):430-437.
8. Centers for Disease Control and Prevention. Psychology of a Crisis. *CRC Crisis + Emergency Risk Communication.* 2019 Update. https://emergency.cdc.gov/cerc/ppt/CERC_Psychology_of_a_Crisis.pdf. Accessed March 2, 2021.

CHAPTER 2

Preparation and Planning

Every aspect of life is handled more effectively when it involves planning. Although preparing for the unknown is difficult, it is possible to minimize the damage by learning from others' experiences. For example, if the weather forecast in your area predicts a Category 4 hurricane will make landfall tomorrow at approximately 6:00 p.m., your knowledge of the destruction that intense storms can inflict helps you prepare for the possible consequences. Your preparation includes ensuring you have insurance coverage, safety protocols, financial arrangements, operational policies, communication procedures, and supply acquisition. What you do not know from first-hand experience you learn from others' experiences.

Whatever the nature of the crisis, everyone should consider general preparations. In this chapter, we focus on preparing your healthcare practice for the unexpected.

BUSINESS CONTINUATION PLANNING

A crisis can threaten a business' ability to continue usual operations or, at minimum, can impede day-to-day performance and hinder business growth. Establishing policies that ensure the business continues in an emergency is a top priority.

How does a typical medical practice continue to render clinical services to patients in a crisis situation? The answer depends on the physical constraints and challenges of the crisis. For example, if a hurricane damages the medical offices, it may be possible to see patients at the hospital or other locations until the primary office is restored. But for that to happen, you need to have a back-up plan already in place.

If your medical practice is in a geographic location where hurricanes or tornados are common, identify a medical office building where you can relocate if necessary. Negotiate with the building management company to have the first option for a temporary space. This may require paying a retainer, but it will be worth the cost to maintain access to your patients. If the facilities are damaged but can be configured temporarily to accommodate patients, work with the building management company for a suitable back-up plan.

Business continuity requires preplanning for the human side as well. Not only must employees be able to function in the temporary accommodations, they must be able to get to and from their workplaces.

During the aftermath of Hurricane Harvey in August 2017, when much of Houston, Texas, was under water, medical facilities in the area had to provide transportation to nurses and staff so they could report to work and provide patient care. Preplanning a strategy for transportation might seem extreme during normal circumstance, but it may be critical to business continuity during adverse times.

More recently, during the COVID-19 pandemic crisis, healthcare providers have had to adjust to new ways of continuing business services, particularly care delivery. Although physicians can treat patients most effectively in person through a clinic visit, during the pandemic, virtual encounters through telehealth offered patient–provider access for which payors now compensate. Consequently, a critical component of business continuity in a medical practice is now telehealth services. Patient access continues and the revenue stream persists. (See Chapter 9 for more information about technology.)

PERSONAL AND FAMILY PREPAREDNESS

The remnants of Hurricane Zeta hit landfall on the Louisiana coastline on October 28, at 3:48 p.m. and came through the metro-Atlanta area, where Coker Group is located, the next morning at 9:35. Hurricane Zeta's high winds caused power outages to 2.6 million customers (about the population of Mississippi) in the southeastern United States, with 984,010 outages reported in Georgia alone.

While this storm was considered mild by all measures, it still required a fair amount of crisis management. Trees and power lines were down, and many homes were without electricity for several days. That meant no power to run appliances, no internet access, and suboptimal cellular coverage. Without a way to communicate or stay informed, it is difficult to address business needs. The result is lost productivity and overall economic and operational disruptions. However, proper planning can mitigate these losses. *Consumer Reports* offers these tips for preparing for such a scenario[1]:

- Ensure all technology is fully charged at all times, such as cellular phones, laptop computers, and other portable devices. Conserve the battery by switching your device to a power-saving setting such as airplane mode or battery-saving mode. Use gas to cook food that will otherwise spoil. Do not forget your gas grill.
- If possible, store frozen and perishable food with friends and family who still have electricity.
- Store containers of ice or frozen water bottles in the refrigerator/ freezer to keep food cold during an extended power outage.
- Keep lanterns available and accessible.
- Purchase battery-operated desk lamps for critical areas.
- If you make your way to a local shelter or library (or any place where there is power), take a power strip to plug in your technology devices for recharging. With a power strip, you can charge multiple devices at once or share the charging station with others.
- If you have a generator, use it safely.

When preparing for a crisis, consider the specific needs of the household. Stock up on non-perishable items that do not require refrigeration. Keep batteries on hand and charged. In areas where storms are frequent, consider buying a generator to maintain partial power. While expensive, generators are a sound investment for your home or business to maintain continuity.

Create an emergency preparedness kit for each family member. Maintain a list of the locations of flashlights, batteries, password summaries, and other crucial items to help you pick up where you left off when the crisis is over. Have a plan that details where to go and how to communicate with family members who are detached during the crisis.

A family emergency plan will provide the security you need to be ready for a problem. Practice the emergency plan with family and household members. Consider sharing your "practice sessions" with other families who live in the same community who need to stay in touch. The same guidance applies to business owners. Share your emergency plans so business continuity is not disrupted when communications are compromised or reduced.

Examples of readiness plans are included at the end of this chapter.

ASSESSING ORGANIZATION VULNERABILITY[2]

Conducting a comprehensive vulnerability assessment before developing a crisis preparedness plan allows the healthcare organization to identify probable and predictable crises and, in some cases, avoid them. Knowing how to plan for and navigate through a crisis is a large part of the solution. Focusing on the realities of a crisis and the healthcare entity's vulnerabilities are therefore an essential part of the preplanning and overall management process.

Healthcare organizations can use the following steps to assess their vulnerability to an organizational crisis and develop a crisis communication plan[3]:

1. Designate a crisis team.
2. Create a vulnerability assessment tool.
3. Analyze results and develop scenarios.
4. Develop a comprehensive crisis communication plan.

Let's examine each of these steps in greater detail.

1. Designate a Crisis Team

A well-organized crisis management team will help ensure the severity of the crisis and its effects on the organization are limited. The team should include individuals who have both experience and maturity within the organization and within their profession, if possible. They should be able to maintain a calm demeanor in crisis situations.

A clear chain of command and well-defined roles within the team is essential, beginning with the CEO, who should be at the head of the crisis team. Other members should include a communications coordinator, spokesperson, and perhaps a safety and security coordinator. A legal representative also may need to be a part of the group. The size of the organization will dictate the size of the crisis team and its overall make-up.

2. Create a Vulnerability Assessment Tool

The organization's ability to evaluate the level of severity of a crisis—in other words, its ability to "anticipate, cope with, resist and recover from the impact of a hazardous event"[4] — is critical to crisis prevention and management. Thus, healthcare organizations should develop an assessment tool that measures their vulnerability to a crisis prior to an incident. This assessment may be implemented in a variety of ways, such as questionnaires, surveys, interviews, and location inspections. Assessing vulnerability falls under the purview of the crisis management team. The assessment may uncover such vulnerabilities as possible data breaches, inadequate backup systems, or even reputational damage (see Chapter 1).

3. Analyze Results and Develop Scenarios

Accountability is an essential aspect of any assessment and preparedness process. The organization must analyze the results of the vulnerability assessment, identify those areas most in need of attention, and develop response plans around scenarios in those critical areas. It is essential to continually analyze the vulnerabilities based on the results of subsequent surveys, interviews, and other input, and thus be better prepared for a crisis.

4. Develop a Comprehensive Crisis Communications Plan

Being able to communicate internally and externally with all stakeholders during a crisis is critical. Without strong and defined communication plans, some people will be uninformed about how the organization is addressing the crisis and may assume the worst. A comprehensive communications plan addresses the scenarios identified in the vulnerability assessment by providing messaging for each situation, including messages tailored for each audience—internal employees, external stakeholders, the news media, and social media.

Developing a Preparedness Plan

Healthcare organizations typically have three types of emergencies to consider: medical, environmental, and violence-related. Having a preparedness plan for each is imperative, as is a response plan that includes action plans, emergency protocols, staff training and equipment and supply back-up.

Medical Emergencies

When creating an emergency plan and responding to medical events, healthcare organizations should focus on such areas as transporting staff and patients to medical offices, transporting patients to the emergency department, and training staff and providers in the emergency response plan so they are ready to swing into action when necessary. While periodic training and retraining may seem like a somewhat extraneous exercise, it's necessary to ensure an efficient and effective response.

Environmental Emergencies

Environmental emergencies can range from hurricanes to chemical spills. Some emergencies can be forecast, such as hurricanes; others offer no advanced notice, such as industrial accidents. Contingency plans should be a part of the overall preplanning process. Knowing what options and alternatives exist due to power outages and lack of other resources are essential to have in place.

Violence-Related Emergencies

These types of crises are unpredictable at best. They may emanate from a disgruntled or disruptive employee or an employee who has personal issues that spill over into the work environment. A disgruntled patient could also be a source of such a crisis.

The unpredictability of these emergencies makes them difficult to plan for, but organizations can be vigilant to some warning signs. For example, a disgruntled employee usually is vocal about his or her unhappiness; employees should be encouraged to confidentially inform the leadership of the organization if they believe the employee may be dangerous to himself/herself or others. Encouraging open dialogue and educating employees about the code of conduct and disciplinary actions that reinforce the organization's commitment to a safe workplace are suitable ways to start addressing these issues.

With certain open-door policies, employees can disclose personal difficulties in confidence. Certain modifications to that employee's working conditions could be a way to proactively avert a greater crisis for the whole organization.

Disgruntled patients or their family members may be difficult to identify; therefore, the organization's entire staff should be aware and have their guard up for warning signs. Unfortunately, sometimes these situations can turn violent, and the employer should be ready to contact law enforcement, isolate the aggressor, and evacuate the premises as quickly as possible. Usually, however, disgruntled patients and/

or their family members can be spoken to in private and given added time to vent (even with the physician). Still, pre-planning for such crises is in order.

It is the responsibility of the owner of the healthcare organization to put emergency response plans in place and include them in the policies and procedures manual of the organization. Leadership is also responsible for training and keeping employees informed of potential crisis situations and how to react to them.

Appendix A, at the end of the book, includes a Master Checklist from the Insurance Institute for Business & Home Safety. Links to forms for documentation of training and maintaining vital information is included in Appendix A. See https://disastersafety.org/wp-content/uploads/2020/09/ofb-ez_Master-Checklist.pdf. The toolkit and forms are at https://disastersafety.org/wp-content/uploads/OFB-EZ_Toolkit_IBHS.pdf. Forms are available for reprint.

SUMMARY

As with most every aspect of running a healthcare organization, preplanning, documentation and training of staff and related parties will significantly mitigate the challenges of any crisis a healthcare organization may face. In this chapter, we have provided examples and further discussion of these items to be mindful and part of the overall organization's infrastructure. Links to forms for documentation are in Appendix A at the end of this book. With these things developed, the healthcare organization will ensure that it can respond to crises effectively.

RESOURCES

1. Haniya R. How to Survive a Prolonged Power Outage. *Consumer Reports*. February 16, 2021. www.consumerreports.org/home-safety/how-to-survive-a-prolonged-power-outage. Accessed April 16, 2021.
2. Homeland Security and Emergency Management. Personal and Family Preparedness. Minnesota Department of Public Safety. https://dps.mn.gov/divisions/hsem/emergency-preparedness/Pages/personal-preparedness.aspx. Accessed April 16, 2021.
3. Deuber KM. Assessing Your Vulnerability: Predict and Prepare for Your Healthcare Organization's Next Crisis. *Beckers Hospital Review*. February 12, 2018. www.beckershospitalreview.com/hr/assessing-your-vulnerability-predict-and-prepare-for-your-healthcare-organization-s-next-crisis.html. Accessed April 16, 2021.

4. Du Y, Ding, Y, Li Z, et al. The Role of Hazard Vulnerability Assessments in Disaster Preparedness and Prevention in China. *Military Med Res*. 2015;2(27). https://doi.org/10.1186/s40779-015-0059-9. https://mmrjournal.biomedcentral.com/articles/10.1186/s40779-015-0059-9#citeas. Accessed April 16, 2021.

CHAPTER 3

Day-to-Day Crisis Management

Planning for a crisis includes outlining ways to address the disruption, regardless of the nature of the event. This chapter considers fundamental aspects of crisis management and serves as an essential guide for dealing with a crisis and its ongoing supervision. We discuss the most effective approaches to managing the medical practice operations day-to-day and into the future.

Faced with an unprecedented health crisis and a growing economic crisis due to the COVID-19 pandemic, it is essential to be proactive, not reactive. Further, it is necessary to lead, not just manage. Leadership in a crisis is not a one-person job that can occur in a vacuum; it is multidimensional. In an *MIT Sloan Management Review*, Eric McNulty, associate director of the National Preparedness Leadership Initiative at Harvard, explains how to follow this approach by emphasizing three points[1]:

1. **Stay true to your purpose.** As a leader, it is essential to know who you are. First, take a step back, take a deep breath, and look at the larger picture to understand how what you see fits into a broader context. Know your strengths and weaknesses. Your experience and education are unique to you. To be successful in a crisis, you need to be grounded and ground your team cognitively, psychologically, and emotionally.

2. **Continually build trust.** Be credible, reliable, always ready to invest in your relationships. Be sure you are here for the greater good, not for self-interest.

3. **Invest in Others.** Talk to your clients, suppliers, and associates to build relationships. Show you care about them as people— their health, economic well-being, all aspects of their lives. Demonstrate that you are committed to a larger goal and that we are all in this together.[1]

Healthcare administration is more than a business; it's a highly technical and personal service industry. You may not have direct authority over patients, but you do have the influence to help them make better decisions and understand the decisions they must make.

The following sections provide detailed guidelines for successful crisis management and are grounded in these points.

ACTIONS TO TAKE BEFORE A DISASTER

Regardless of the type of disaster or crisis, it pays to be prepared. Here are seven steps[2] to consider.

1. **Make copies and backup files.** Losing critical files not only results in the loss of critical information and answers, it also results in inefficiencies as processes are no longer documented and continuity is harder to maintain as personnel turns over.

2. **Have an evacuation plan in place.** Trying to organize people to evacuate a building safely and promptly amid a crisis event can be chaotic. The chaos compounds with the introduction of other variables, like patients needing medical care. Having an evacuation plan that addresses all contingencies is critical.

3. **Test your plan.** Like anything, practice makes perfect. Periodic crisis plan rehearsals help remove the emotion of a crisis event and prevent people from freezing or making a wrong decision in an emotion-charged event.

4. **Be prepared to work remotely.** Today's technology enables new forms of communication to accommodate mobile workforces. Launching new modalities like telehealth is a way to keep revenue streams intact. Remote solutions do not just happen, however. They need to be planned so they can be implemented with as little interruption as possible when necessary.

5. **Have a tested backup plan ready to go.** It is unlikely that things will go according to plan during a crisis event, so it is necessary to have a tested backup plan for when circumstances dictate the need to deviate from the original plan.

6. **Review your insurance.** There is a lot to be done following a crisis event. Researching your insurance constraints and options should not be among them. Understand your plans' details prior

to a crisis event to minimize the lead time associated with enacting insurance policies. (See Chapter 12 for discussion of insurance considerations.)

7. **Stay on top of your receivables.** Patient-responsible balances are a growing industry trend. A crisis can affect your customers' ability to pay, which disrupts your business's cash flow. Stay on top of your receivables to maximize the cash flow needed to fund post-crisis events. (See Chapter 7 for more information related to financial matters.)

OFFICE POLICIES AND TRAINING

A quick and effective initial response during times of crisis will, at a minimum, help navigate the practice through uncertainty; it may save lives. According to ready.gov,[3] an official disaster and preparation website of the United States government, protective actions for life safety include:

1. Evacuation: Includes a warning system, exit strategy, and log of employees and visitors to ensure everyone has gotten out safely.
2. Sheltering: Includes a warning system and designated safe area for sheltering—the strongest part of the building, such as basements or interior rooms.
3. Shelter-in-place: Includes a warning system to warn occupants to move to the core of the building.
4. Lockdown: Includes directions to seek refuge in a room, lock doors, and remain silent.

Every organization should have an emergency plan that includes these protective actions with policies to follow as a crisis hits. Key to the guidelines found within an organization's emergency plan is a list of clear operating procedures that are easy to follow. This list is foundational so that existing policies that are already familiar to the staff can be expanded and/or supplemented with additional requirements necessary for crisis times. Policies for physical disasters and unforeseen crises can be expanded only so far within the existing policy infrastructure. At some point these policies will need to be supplemented with new ones that are independent of anything already in place. As these new policies are incorporated within the emergency plan, perform the risk assessment to find gaps that can be filled with additional procedures. Specific policies that are likely to be identified may include:

1. Communication guidelines to help staff understand how to notify office administration if/when affected.
2. Protocols regarding patient communication about remote patient monitoring and digital health tools.
3. HIPAA (Health Insurance Portability and Accountability) compliance of communication guidelines.

DEALING WITH A CRISIS AND ITS ONGOING MANAGEMENT

Renowned management consultant Peter Drucker wrote in the *Effective Executive*[4] that the executive becomes a prisoner of events without an action plan. Below are essential steps in an action plan to deal with a crisis within a practice setting.

1. **Establish a clear chain of command.** Establish a clear chain of command and rapid response process to ensure swift, decisive action. In case of a physical disaster, your response team must be charged with evaluating the situation daily with safety consideration for patients, clinicians, and staff. The team must be prepared for what to do ahead of time rather than caught up in real-time decision making. This preparation will mitigate pressure-induced errors and lessen the emotional toll associated with the situation. A prepared staff is a resilient staff—an intangible asset that will serve organizations well during times of crisis.

2. **Have a social media strategy addressed within the emergency plan.** Social media is a powerful tool that can help manage communication with patients, staff, suppliers, and regulatory bodies such as Centers for Medicare & Medicaid Services (CMS). Plan for the ways your practice can use social media in the event of a disaster and document it in your practice's emergency plan.

3. **Create an "immediate needs" checklist.** Crisis events may prompt flexible regulatory guidelines; however, absent any waivers, there will still be some level of mandatory adherence to requirements to ensure proper standards of care. Create a checklist of minimum requirements acceptable to payors to support

Current Procedural Terminology (CPT) coding and continue practice cash flow.

4. **Manage workflow.** Refer to state and federal guidelines for insights to incorporate for calendar planning related to patient outreach to reschedule appointments and procedures that may have been delayed or canceled due to the crisis.

5. **Plan for employee flex and hours.** Cash flow challenges may force your practice to face tough decisions about employee furloughs or cutting non-essential employees. Proper workflow management may help mitigate the need to invoke such drastic measures. Realistically, adjusting work hours may keep the practice functioning properly, serving as an essential element to monitor for successful crisis management.

6. **Utilize digital health tools.** Telehealth and remote monitoring may help your practice provide care outside of the confines of a doctor's office. Understanding that these are new modalities of care that carry specific considerations, reimbursement rules, and regulatory considerations, the American Medical Association (AMA) has developed a quick guide to help physician practices understand telehealth flexibilities amid the COVID-19 pandemic available at www.ama-assn.org/practice-management/digital/ama-telehealth-quick-guide. It is a helpful guide that can provide tenants for ongoing support.

7. **Assess current and future supply needs.** During the initial stages of the COVID-19 crisis, unusual and unforeseen circumstances arose, notably in keeping a proper level of personal protective equipment (PPE) to combat the mounting problem. Consult Centers for Disease Control (CDC) tools for "Guidance for the Selection and Use of Personal Protective Equipment in Healthcare Settings"[5] to understand the proper PPE to maintain the inventory of and/or the ability to acquire the appropriate PPE quickly. Waiting until the PPE is in demand will make it infinitely harder to obtain it quickly and as needed when crises strike.

SUMMARY

The information in this chapter provides the actions to take before a disaster occurs. It presents the case for establishing office policies and the subsequent training for implementing the procedures during and after a crisis. Lastly, it serves as a guide to dealing with a crisis and its ongoing management. These guidelines are developed in more detail in the remainder of this book.

RESOURCES

1. McNulty EJ. Leading Through a Crisis Day by Day. *MIT Sloan Management Review.* April 28, 2020. https://sloanreview.mit.edu/audio/leading-through-a-crisis-day-by-day. Accessed December 4, 2020.
2. Moran B. 7 Steps You Need to Take Before Disaster Strikes. American Express. September 26, 2013. https://www.americanexpress.com/en-us/business/trends-and-insights/articles/7-steps-you-need-to-take-before-disaster-strikes. Accessed December 4, 2020.
3. U.S. Government. Emergency Response Plan. Ready.gov. www.ready.gov/business/implementation/emergency. Accessed December 4, 2020.
4. Drucker P F. *The Effective Executive.* New York: HarperBusiness Essentials, 2002.
5. Centers for Disease Control and Prevention. Protecting Healthcare Personnel. https://www.cdc.gov/hai/prevent/ppe.html. Accessed December 4, 2020.

CHAPTER 4

Communication Techniques During and After the Crisis

A key to effective leadership in a crisis is ensuring all stakeholders are confident in your ability to maintain control during uncertain times. Communication—both internal and external—is critical trust that will extend far beyond the conclusion of the actual crisis period, creating a system of transparency, and building loyalty.

It is important to note that while communication is critical during an organizational crisis, the recommendations and guidance offered here are always relevant, regardless of the organization or the circumstances. Exceptional leaders are effective communicators who create an environment that fosters stability and support in good times and in bad.

Leaders should also recognize that their feelings come through in their communications. Those who do not have a level of emotional intelligence can undermine their communication with subliminal or nonverbal messages. Alternatively, some leaders are highly compassionate and avoid saying what needs to be said for fear of upsetting someone. Both instances are equally dangerous to an organization. Therefore, leaders must practice effective communication strategies in their day-to-day interactions rather than waiting for a crisis situation when their communication may not achieve the desired results.

During times of crisis, leaders must ensure they are confident and direct, while still maintaining a level of compassion and empathy for their staff, peers, and patients. In the following sections, we outline the critical requirements of effective communication.

ENSURE THE MESSAGE IS CLEAR

One of the most frustrating results of poor communication is the feeling that the recipient is even more confused or concerned after the message is delivered. Again, whether in crisis or not, people look to the leaders for advice and insight, and it is critical to impart a sense of confidence in the message you are relaying.

When the message is difficult to deliver, leaders may skirt the truth or answer questions with vague responses. While nonspecific responses may be more comfortable to deliver, the lack of clarity may cause more pain in the long-term. Don't be dishonest when you don't know the answer to a question; admit that you don't have enough information to speak to the point, but provide reassurance that you will seek the information requested.

For example, consider the way leadership responded to the COVID-19 pandemic. During the initial months, one of the most oft-expressed complaints was that information and recommendations changed rapidly. While this is true, the primary issue was that recommendations and information were based on an incomplete set of facts. It would have been best to admit the lack of solid information while being positive and forthright about the recommendations that did come from verifiable data (even if those data changed later).

Overall, whatever is said must be communicated with authority, ensuring no misunderstanding or vagueness. It may be best to draft a few talking points before an important or sensitive meeting, ensuring you hit each issue before the conclusion of the session and holding yourself to those truths.

INFUSE HUMANITY

While being direct is important, it is equally critical to ensure you approach a crisis with humanity—specifically, consideration and compassion for others, and especially those you lead. It is easy as a leader to look at the "big picture" versus the day-to-day at your organization, creating a disconnect between your decisions and how they affect your employees. While it is your role to lead the organization, when you recognize that it may result in some personal sacrifices and/or losses and show kindness, those affected will accept the message in a more favorable light.

We can relate this to a provider's bedside manner. It is how the provider delivers difficult news that makes them stand out and builds rapport.

If your natural inclination is not to lead with empathy, consider practicing these strategies:

- **Listen first, speak second.** Allow your employees time to voice their concerns and frustrations. Respond to their points; do not merely gloss over them in a rush to deliver your message. Take notes as they are speaking and address their points directly through your future messaging and decision making.
- **Be vulnerable and personal.** Address how the crisis is affecting you personally, ensuring you first address your inherent biases and potential privilege. Be mindful that others may suffer more loss than you, and be humble about your circumstances. This approach will create a personal connection, and it also will create a space for them to respond in kind.
- **Allow your body language to help convey the message.** Leaders can create a more open dialogue by changing the way they are sitting, for example. Move out from behind your desk and speak with your audience, not to them, at their level. Remove all distractions and give them undivided attention. Lean in when listening and display your emotions on your face. These mannerisms may seem simple, but they will be more impactful than your words.
- **Ask how you can help.** We often are so focused on the message we are trying to deliver that we miss opportunities to drive value back into the organization. Responses to asking employees "What can we be doing better to support you?" may open your eyes to easy "wins" or areas that you might be overlooking from a higher level. But be careful not to promise something you cannot deliver.

Allowing compassion to infuse your dialogue can significantly improve how you are perceived. Ensure you impart understanding from the top-down, creating a culture of empathy and support throughout the organization.

BUILD TRUST

Trust is critical for success in a crisis; thus, you must begin building it now. Ensure you are consistently approaching leadership decisions in the best way to instill trust. This will create a foundation for your employees to be faithful and supportive, even when the situation seems ominous.

One of the most significant healthcare leadership issues is the lack of transparency between administration and staff, including providers. To discourage the attitude that leaders make decisions behind closed doors and rarely provide the full story, allow your organization's employees into the decision-making process. Keep them informed of developing situations and allow for input from all ranks. Provide the background for decisions and ensure that there is a rationale behind them.

Adopt a semi open-door policy. While a fully open-door system may not be reasonable or even beneficial, set times that staff knows they can meet with you and discuss their concerns; ensure this time remains protected on your calendar. Coordinating ongoing operations in your organization enables you to quickly mitigate issues as they arise versus addressing them when they become a large-scale problem. Maintain confidentiality at all costs as you work discreetly to address employees' concerns. If you believe individual employees are not taking advantage of the access policy, set a one-on-one meeting with them to encourage feedback. Additionally, if you think certain employees are taking advantage, work with other leaders to find ways to address their issues and preemptively set times to meet with them.

A common complaint from employees across all industries is that there is a lot of discussion about problems, but they are rarely followed up on and effectively addressed. This is prevalent in healthcare, where providers often protest the number of meetings they must attend without seeing any real change. While it is impossible to tackle all issues that arise in these sessions, any action items agreed upon must be swiftly executed. Nothing demoralizes employees more than having made their grievances known but never seeing any leadership response.

One of the quickest ways to build trust is to tackle negative issues head-on. While there are specific confidentiality issues and public relations considerations, rumors spread quickly in an organization and leadership should remain in front of these issues. Address what can be addressed and assure your organization that you are aware and in control. This action will set a precedent that you are deeply in tune with your organization and that employees should have confidence that problems will be addressed swiftly and tactfully.

Developing trust takes time and consistency but losing faith can be quick and immediate. It is easy to roll back some policies during a crisis, but doing so negates all trust you have worked so diligently to foster.

BE A MORAL AUTHORITY

Moral authority as it pertains to leadership in an organization has two components: The first component is having the company's and its stakeholders' best interests in mind and consistently making efforts to improve all outcomes, even if you don't always succeed. The second is aligning what you *do* with what you *say*.

1. Having the best interests of the company and its stakeholders at heart and consistently trying to improve outcomes for all. This ties to integrity and genuineness. Does your staff believe that every decision you make is made with them in mind? Or, do they think you have ulterior, potentially self-benefiting motives? People are incredibly perceptive when it comes to this area and typically can ascertain your true intentions. Thus, before each decision, ensure you align with your organization's values and priorities and defend each decision with that response.

2. Aligning what you do with what you say. One of the quickest ways leaders can undermine their message is through contradictory actions. As employees look to you for guidance, your actions must align with the message you are sending — especially during a crisis, when your response creates a ripple effect throughout the organization. Ensure your actions are consistent and align with the outcomes you have set forth in your messaging.

Consistency is never more critical than in a crisis when the organization is looking to you for guidance on how to behave and move forward. During the COVID-19 pandemic, Delta Air Lines CEO Ed Bastian showed his employees his dedication to weathering the storm by announcing he would forego his salary for six months. This move created support and trust that his next steps would benefit the company he served. In fact, after announcing widespread pay cuts among managers at the start of the pandemic, Delta subsequently paid managers bonuses to help make up for the pay cuts.

Moral authority can be the mark (or demise) of a leader. It is more about who you are rather than what your position entails. It is not something you can personally create—it must be bestowed upon you by those you lead. To improve your moral authority, omit entitlement from your internal dialogue, define your moral obligations, and consider all employees equally crucial from the top down.

CONTROL YOUR EMOTIONS

Controlling a situation begins with controlling emotions, keeping a calm exterior, and speaking in a tempered tone. While leaders must lean into their compassionate side, they cannot allow their emotions to take over the conversation. Further, as tensions rise during a crisis, leaders must appear to be fully collected in their thoughts and actions.

Outbursts, especially negative ones, can cause staff to feel uncertain about your ability to navigate the situation at hand. Also remember that communication is more than talking; ensure your body language conveys confidence and calmness.

If a situation becomes particularly stressful, take a break from the conversation, and thoughtfully consider how you want to respond. Don't leave the discussion entirely; rather, sit back and listen to the others while you formulate your next statements. You may even suggest the group members do the same. Remain mindful of how you control this situation. Ensure heated discussions do not spin out of control and don't enter the throes of debate.

As a leader, you must model how to act. Always remain professional—even when others around you may not be acting in kind. This allows you to reshape the dynamic and create a sense of security, regardless of the crisis at hand.

SUMMARY

Each of the four points is critical to developing practical communication skills and each is relevant before, during, and after an organizational crisis. So, what *should* change during a crisis?

First, while these skills are always important, they are even more so during a crisis, so evaluate your adeptness with each and improve where needed.

Second, amplify your communication. Speak with your employees often and repeat the essential points. While repetition may seem redundant, it ensures you are not misunderstood or not heard.

Finally, ensure important messages are shared through a variety of sources. It is easy to rely on carefully crafted emails, but it is vital to deliver your points in multiple mediums during a crisis.

Mastering your communication skills helps you maintain control of your organization and ensures all stakeholders trust and know they can rely on you.

CHAPTER 5

Leadership in Crisis Management

Stories abound of leaders who have faced crises and come out on top. Nancy Koehn, in her research, studied the stories of five leaders (Abraham Lincoln, Ernest Shackleton, Frederick Douglass, Dietrich Bonhoeffer, and Rachel Carson) and then shared the details of the real-life crises each of them faced, how they managed to accept their shortcomings and persevere in the face of impending disaster.

In the opening paragraphs of her book *Forged in Crisis*, Koehn writes, "Read these stories and get to work. The world has never needed you and other real leaders more than it does now."[1] With that charge in mind, this chapter scrutinizes the "how to" of managing through effective leadership during a crisis. It also considers the qualities of both administrative and physician leadership that effectively address an emergency of any nature.

QUALITIES OF EFFECTIVE LEADERS

Research by Everly et al. indicates that effective leaders exhibit four characteristics in times of crisis, as listed in Figure 5.1.[2]

Vision for the Future

An interesting study examined what happened to British Petroleum leaders and employees in the aftermath of the 2010 Gulf of Mexico oil spill. The study found that employees had varied reactions to the crisis. Some doubted BP and lost their faith in the organization, while others became even more committed to BP and increased their efforts to support it. One of the single greatest differentiating factors between these two sets of employees was how much they heard from leaders about where the organization was going next and how much they were engaged to actively support that vision.

FIGURE 5.1. Qualities of Effective Leaders

Many of those who lacked this exposure to the key messages and were not involved in the clean-up process ended up ambivalent or, even worse, feeling disconnected from the organization. Conversely, those employees whose leaders included them in the crisis response, helped them understand where things were heading, and explained the employee's role in supporting the organization's commitment to rectifying the wrong fell into the other, more engaged category.

This research supports the belief that employees do not need to merely hear some sunnier version of the current reality; they need to understand how leaders interpret what is happening during a crisis, what direction leaders are setting to create stability, and what their own role is in achieving that vision.[3]

Effective leadership during a crisis requires these components in equal measure—being able to set a clear, achievable vision for the future as well as engaging people in helping achieve that vision. One of the realities of a crisis is that knowing what vision to cast is often incredibly difficult. Living with an ever-changing series of events, a great unknown about what is going to happen next, and an unclear picture of the resources available to effect change makes knowing where to start a challenge, much less what the future needs to hold.

However, in these times, people look to their leaders for a unifying vision for the future. For example, amid the uncertainty of the COVID-19 pandemic, one hospital chief executive officer (CEO) decided that the vision for his organization was going to be that no caregiver would perish because of contracting COVID-19 at work. This clear, achievable vision was relatable to everyone working in the hospital, from the front-line physicians to the environmental services technicians. Additionally, it created a call to action for every person to be diligent in their processes and behaviors so as not to contaminate themselves, their colleagues, or their patients.

Visions like these may apply to the immediate future, especially in situations when uncertainties abound and it is difficult to extend past that day or week, or they may be a longer-term vision. Regardless, during a crisis, people need to see and understand where things are heading and have leaders who will, with their support, get them there.

Decisiveness

In their research, Panos et al. state, "The approach of the health crisis manager has to be meticulous; his thoughts must be algorithmic; **decisions and actions have to be coordinated** and expectations must be realistic." In addition, they note, "The manager needs to demonstrate the **ability to decide and act** without revealing emotional tension that may be related to the events." And finally, "Flexibility, avoidance of dogmatism, adaptability to the circumstances and **rapid decisional capacity are fundamental qualities of health crisis managers.**"[4] This belief is widely accepted; however, the challenge is that when forced with a difficult decision (as is often the case in the face of a crisis), many leaders become afflicted with cognitive dissonance.

The psychology of cognitive dissonance began with the investigations of Leon Festinger, who while on the faculty at the University of Minnesota, studied a cult that was preparing for the end of the world. He was interested in seeing how the believers would react when the world did not get destroyed by a flood.

Festinger observed that some believers owned up to their incorrect belief, but others (specifically those who were incredibly committed to the cult and staunch in their beliefs about the coming end of ages), altered their version of events to assert that their faith had saved the world. These believers shared their opinions widely with the media and bystanders and were seemingly unperturbed by their own change in messaging.

Festinger understood these actions from a psychological perspective, and believed they supported his developing theory of cognitive dissonance, which is based on the concept that people need to keep their beliefs and behaviors aligned, or they become internally conflicted. This concept explains, then, why the most deeply committed group of believers changed their version of the events leading up to December 21, 1954: to ensure their newfound *belief* (that their acts saved the world from demise) and their *behaviors* (selling their possessions, relocating to Illinois, and being part of this cult) would then be consistent.

Festinger went on to Stanford University, where he began more extensive study into his theory. Experiments there (including one of his best known, in which study subjects were asked to lie about their interest and enjoyment in completing repetitive, menial tasks), confirmed and helped to better refine the cognitive dissonance theory.

In times of crisis, cognitive dissonance can challenge a leader's ability to be decisive. As a crisis unfolds, many courses of potential action may present themselves; some may look good, and some may look bad. But as leaders begin to earnestly sift through these options, they may realize that taking one course eliminates the possibility of taking another, and therein lies the beginning of their cognitive dissonance.

Faced with the belief they can make the correct decision, and then recognizing the action they take may prove this to be incorrect, leaders often stumble. Since most humans do not enjoy this feeling of cognitive dissonance, they start to find reasons to not pursue courses of action rather than merely selecting one assuredly and pursuing it actively. It is this process of mentally (and sometimes, operationally) "crossing off" the alternatives that takes time, and thus, makes the decisiveness necessary amid a crisis more difficult for some leaders to achieve.

For example, I have seen many first-time CEOs freeze when needing to decide whether to pay a ransomware demand or trying to determine how much information to share when asked in a public forum about a recurring and adverse clinical outcome within their facility. However, as noted above, even when much is unknown, it is important for a leader to use the information they have at the time and take swift and decisive action.

Of course, it is also important to as quickly as possible determine if that was the correct course—"fail fast," as the adage goes. (In systems design, a fail-fast system is one that immediately reports at its interface any condition that is likely to indicate a failure. Such designs often check the system's state at several points in an operation, so any failures can be detected early.)

However, being decisive at the outset often allows more time for failure and course correction; this time is not afforded if there is an initial delay in taking any action whatsoever.

Effective Communication

While Chapter 4 more fully examines communication techniques to be used during and after a crisis, it is worth reiterating here that the perceived effectiveness of a leader's communication during a crisis often differentiates them from being a "good leader" and a "bad leader." What, then, makes a leader's communication "effective?" The work of Fischhoff et al. indicates to be considered "adequate," communication should address three things:[5]

1. The communication includes the information needed for effective decision-making,
2. Users can access that information, and
3. Users can comprehend what they access.

One commonly cited example of ineffective communication is the City of New Orleans during Hurricane Katrina. The analysis of Cole and Fellows concludes that "inadequate clarity, insufficient credibility, and a failure to properly adapt to critical audiences resulted in a failure of . . . crisis communication" during one of the most damaging environmental disasters within the United States.[6] From their findings, as well as the complementary standards set independently by Fischoff et al., several key lessons emerge.

First, information needs to be adapted to its audience. In healthcare organizations in crisis, this may mean adapting the message when presenting it to various departments. This adaptation requires consistent, yet differentiated messaging for the finance department, members of the medical staff, and the executive leadership team, as an example.

Second, crisis communication must be clear if action is required. During Hurricane Katrina, evacuation notices were characterized by language such as "precautionary," "voluntary," "recommended," "highly recommended," and "highly suggested," when in reality, by that time, language indicating that evacuation was "mandatory" was sorely needed to ensure as many people as possible left the area to avoid harm.[7] This belies the importance of including facts and explicitly clear instructions when action is required, so individuals can make their own informed decisions.

And, finally, communication must reach its intended audience for it be effective. This is the reason so many crisis communication plans include the advance development of a contact repository, which includes stakeholders' home phone numbers, alternate mobile numbers, personal email addresses, emergency contact information, and in more recent years, their social media handles.

It is also why some healthcare organizations are creating password-protected portals on web-based social networking platforms, so employees have another readily accessible (and sometimes even bi-directional) method of communication when traditional methods such as physical signage or in-person messages are not possible given the circumstances of the emergency.

These numerous and myriad alternative methods to reach people ensure that, when necessary, communication is accessible and ultimately received by those who need it.

Moral Authority

"Managers are *given* responsibility; leaders *earn* respect," John C. Maxwell states. Maxwell notes that leaders earn this respect in several ways, including the consistent exemplification of moral authority. He discusses moral authority at length in his book, *LeaderShift*, and associated writings.[8] Here, he specifically notes that leaders who earn moral authority do so by being consistent in three areas: competence, courage, and character.

1. **Competence** is the ability to lead well. Making smart decisions, knowing your people, understanding your field, and committing to personal growth are all examples of competence. Leaders who demonstrate that they know what they are doing—and that they learn from their mistakes—establish themselves as leaders worth following.

2. **Courage** is moving forward in the face of fear. Courage is not the absence of fear, but the presence of mind to act when afraid. Every leader needs courage to make hard decisions, implement needed changes, and cast vision.
3. **Character** is being bigger on the inside than the outside. Leaders of character know that who they are is more than what they achieve. Character is a commitment to continual growth in the areas of integrity, authenticity, humility, and love.[9]

So why is it that moral authority is one of the principal qualities of an effective leader? As opposed to positional authority, in which individuals are required, by location on an organizational chart or their title, to honor their chain of command, moral authority results when inspired people *choose* to respect their leader.

This concept of following someone because I want to, not because I am told to, creates longer lasting and stronger ties between the employee and leader. However, one of the challenges of moral authority is that, like trust, once it is lost, it is often quite difficult to regain; unlike positional authority, there is no "requirement" for the respect that had once been assigned to the leader.[10] This is seen in situations when a leader (and often the organization by association) is the subject of a reputational crisis (examples include extramarital affairs, embezzling from the company, or even receiving compensation significantly greater than the rest of the workforce within the same organizations), and they lose the confidence of their constituents. Thus, while difficult to earn and potentially easier to lose, moral authority remains one of the most notable characteristics of an effective leader.

MANAGEMENT PRINCIPLES FOR ADMINISTRATIVE AND PHYSICIAN LEADERS

Recent initiatives implemented at Johns Hopkins Medicine focus on promoting and enhancing effective leadership in crisis. Through nine guiding principles, leaders (with a focus on frontline leaders) were educated on how to build their own resilience and lead others in a manner that minimized the negative impacts of crisis.[2] These principles are applicable to both administrative and physician leadership and are summarized in Figure 5.2.

FIGURE 5.2. Effective Leadership in Crisis

Leadership Principle	Application
1. Structure is the antidote for chaos.	Create routines upon which people can depend. This may include daily huddles, email updates distributed at a specific time each day, or other recurrent communications.
2. Listen before you speak.	As opposed to assuming you have the answers, allow employees to first share what is on their minds. Use open-ended questions to solicit feedback and better understand the issues at hand.
3. Information is an antidote for anxiety.	Information comes in three forms: anticipatory guidance (what may happen), explanatory guidance (what happened and why it happened), and prescriptive guidance (recommendations or mandates for action). Leaders need to provide information in the applicable form(s) as much as possible. Remember, if you are not providing the information, employees will be getting it elsewhere.
4. Transparent, timely, and truthful communication is essential to maintain credibility.	Message frequently and use repetitive messages. Anticipate questions and try to answer them in advance. If you do not have an answer, be honest in saying so, but follow up with when and/or how that information will be provided.
5. People trust actions, not words.	Do what you say you are going to do. Let your own actions be an example for how people should act.
6. Empowerment is an antidote for feeling out of control.	Help stakeholders develop an increased sense of control by soliciting their feedback. Overtly act on the applicable ideas.
7. The perception of support is the antidote for isolation.	Be seen frequently. Walk around and check in with people, even informally, to both listen to their issues and demonstrate your commitment to supporting them.
8. Cohesive groups do better with stress and challenges than non-cohesive groups.	Create connectedness through the reinforcement of a shared vision. Acknowledge, with gratitude, the contributions of all team members.
9. The moment of absolute certainty may never arise.	Be decisive when action is needed, even if you do not have all the information you would like.

SUMMARY

Effective leadership has been correlated with increased resilience and potentially lower incidence of psychological casualties in people ensnared in crisis.[11] If for these reasons alone, it is extremely important. However, not all leaders are effective in crisis, and it is often difficult to determine their likelihood of success until they are in the throes of disaster. Thus, education regarding the qualities and actions of effective leaders is the first step in ultimately developing these necessary skills and ensuring their emergence when crisis strikes.

RESOURCES

1. Koehn N. 2017. *Forged in Crisis: The Power of Courageous Leadership in Turbulent Times*. New York: Simon & Schuster, Inc.; 2017.
2. Everly G, Wu A, Cumpsty-Fowler C, Dang D, & Potash J. Leadership Principles to Decrease Psychological Casualties in COVID-19 and Other Disasters of Uncertainty. *Disaster Medicine and Public Health Preparedness*. October 2020;1-3. doi:10.1017/dmp.2020.395.
3. Petriglieri JL. Co-creating Relationship Repair: Pathways to Reconstructing Destabilized Organizational Identification. *Administrative Science Quarterly*. 60(3):518–557. doi:10.1177/0001839215579234.
4. Panos E. Crisis Management in the Health Sector; Qualities and Characteristics of Health Crisis Managers. *International Journal of Caring Sciences*. September–December 2009; 2(3).
5. Fischhoff B, Brewer NT, Downs JS, Eds. Communicating Risks and Benefits: An Evidence-Based User's Guide. Washington, DC: U. S. Department of Health and Human Services, Food and Drug Administration; 2018. Accessed May 27, 2021.
6. Cole, TW, Fellows KL. Risk Communication Failure: A Case Study of New Orleans and Hurricane Katrina *Southern Communication Journal*. 2008; 73(3):211-228. doi: 10.1080/10417940802219702.
7. Select Bipartisan Committee. (2006, February 15). A Failure of Initiative: Final Report of the Select Bipartisan Committee to Investigate the Preparation for and Response to Hurricane Katrina. 109th Congress, 2nd Session, U.S. Government Printing Office.
8. Maxwell JC. *LeaderShift*. New York: HarperCollins Leadership; 2019.
9. Maxwell JC. Become a Leader Others Want to Follow. blog. February 5, 2019. www.johnmaxwell.com/blog/become-a-leader-others-want-to-follow/. Accessed May 27, 2021.
10. Haimes YY. *Risk Modeling of Interdependent Complex Systems of Systems: Theory and Practice. Risk Analysis*. 2018;38(1).

11. Brooks, SK, Rubin, GJ, Greenberg, N. Traumatic Stress Within Disaster-exposed Occupations: Overview of the Literature and Suggestions for the Management of Traumatic Stress in the Workplace. *British Medical Bulletin*. 2019;129(1):25-34. doi: 10.1093/bmb/ldy040.

CHAPTER 6

Crisis Mitigation

The adage "the best offense is a good defense" has been credited to many different people, from President George Washington to football coach Knute Rockne, to basketball legend Michael Jordan. The intent of the message is usually to convey that preparation is key to achieving a successful outcome. In many ways, this message is directly applicable to healthcare organizations in times of crisis. Without a "good defense" developed through adequate preparation, a crisis is apt to have more impact.

This chapter focuses on minimizing the effects of a crisis within a medical practice or other healthcare delivery organization, including ways to address issues quickly and thereby limit their adverse effects. It considers preparedness (as initially discussed in Chapter Two) and builds on that factor with three other essential crisis mitigation strategies that collectively can positively direct the outcome of the crisis at hand.

MINIMIZING THE POTENTIAL IMPACT OF A CRISIS

The National Academies of Sciences, Engineering, and Medicine released guidance[1] regarding ways to reduce natural disasters' effects on communities. This body of work emphasizes the importance of four critical areas of action: awareness, education, preparedness, and prediction and warning systems. While intended to consider natural disasters, these areas of action are applicable to a much broader array of potential disasters. Accordingly, a discussion of each of these four key areas follows.

Awareness

Awareness is a consciousness of a fact or situation. It requires active engagement and is a critical precursor to understanding. Awareness empowers people to make changes by addressing areas of opportunity or building on areas of strength.

Awareness is the first step in healthcare crisis management because it emphasizes the reality that any organization is vulnerable. *Becker's Hospital Review* released their perspective on the five most significant security breaches in 2020[2] for healthcare organizations, which included a breach at Inova that affected one million people and a cyberattack at UVM Health Network that infected 5,000 computers that lasted more than 40 days and cost the health system $63 million in lost revenue and extra expenses (more than $1.5 million per day in financial impact).

These types of crises merely scratch the surface of possible risks to healthcare organizations, and yet, they never cross the minds of many people. Only by raising awareness of all the potential ways healthcare organizations can find themselves in crisis can system leaders begin preparations to ensure that when a crisis arises, they are ready.

The work of Fischhoff et al.[3] indicates that effective communication meets one or more goals, including:

1. Shares information.
2. Changes beliefs.
3. Changes behaviors.

In this first step of crisis mitigation (*awareness*), leaders should focus their communication solely on sharing information with the intent of providing knowledge about the variety of crises that can impact the organization and beginning a process that will ultimately yield better critical thinking, more self-control, and improved decision making. This is not to imply that the two other goals of effective communication (changing beliefs and changing behaviors) are not critical; it is simply that when considering where to begin in the crisis mitigation process, the first thought should be toward increasing *awareness* among key stakeholders.

Education

Albert Einstein is often credited with saying "Education is not the learning of facts, but the training of the mind to think." The purpose of education as a critical step to crisis mitigation, then, is to train stakeholders (including formal and informal leaders) how to think so when a crisis arises, they can make decisions quickly even in the face of high anxiety and incomplete information.

The United States government created a resource guide relative to crisis preparation and response that includes information sheets, toolkits, guides, and plans to address a range of emergencies such as active shooter, cyberattack, earthquake, financial emergency, novel pandemic, and power outage.

The information sheet[4] for each includes instructions for what to do before, during, and after the emergency. Distributing and routinely referencing these information sheets is an excellent way for medical practices to educate their staff and physicians regarding how crises can be impactful, underscore to what extent they can disrupt business operations, and delineate the types of planning that need to start immediately.

Concerning the work of Fischhoff et al., referenced above[3], these actions address the second goal of effective communication: changing beliefs. Through the education process, people become aware of the potential for a crisis rather than continuing to believe that they and their organization are immune. Much as awareness is a precursor to understanding, this change in views is necessary to changing behaviors.

Although *patient* education is a critical component of overall crisis management, it is secondary to internal practice education. This is because patient education typically is focused on *outcomes* (i.e., what action is expected of them in the case of an emergency) instead of *preparation*. Due to the highly regulated healthcare industry and its potential effects on the public's health and wellness, we consider the practice's *risk* communication (rather than *public relations* communication, which often requires less accuracy and can be slanted) to be of the highest value during the pre-crisis stage. Patients are then the downstream recipients of the plans that the practice makes.

Preparedness

Chapter Two outlines the need for appropriate preparation in anticipation of a crisis. Below, we reinforce practical and actionable steps to ensure adequate preparation, including those endorsed by the Federal Emergency Management Agency (FEMA).[5] FEMA's "12 Ways to Prepare" for disasters are outlined in Figure 6.1.

FIGURE 6.1. FEMA's 12 Ways to Prepare

☐ Sign up for Alerts and Warnings	☐ Make a Plan	☐ Save for a Rainy Day	☐ Practice Emergency Drills	☐ Test Family Communication Plan	☐ Safeguard Documents
☐ Plan with Neighbors	☐ Make Your Home Safer	☐ Know Evacuation Routes	☐ Assemble or Update Supplies	☐ Get Involved in Your Community	☐ Document and Insure Property

Using FEMA's "12 Ways to Prepare" as the basis, we have adapted these steps to best align with a medical practice's needs.

1. Sign up for alerts and warnings.

Individuals can sign up for alerts and notifications, such as those available through local and national emergency management offices (see specific examples later in this chapter) and/or leaders can connect with the people within their organization. Never has the concept of "management by walking around" carried more potential benefit than in its ability to identify problems before they develop into a driving force for a crisis. By interacting with stakeholders at all levels, in all roles, and across all departments, leaders can learn more about what is happening and be able to effectively take their staff's pulse. Knowing when people seem stressed and learning what issues they see as important are essentially "signing up" to receive warnings of plausible matters as they arise.

2. Make a plan.

As is noted throughout this book, planning, documenting, and widely sharing are critical tasks for leaders during a crisis and during noncrisis times. This plan should address the actions to be taken before, during, and after the problem; identify the crisis response team members; outline communication strategies (including sample language for various hazards); and provide complete contact information for key stakeholders.

3. Ensure access to financial support.

Regardless of the type of crisis an organization experiences, one of the most likely outcomes is financial expenditure. Whether it is fortifying a clinical building against a natural disaster or managing through the loss in revenue incurred from lower volume due to a reputation issue, the economic impact of a crisis can become overwhelming if a practice does not have money available to sustain itself in the emergency.

Because medical practices (particularly independent practices) often distribute all proceeds annually to minimize their tax implications, many do not keep significant liquid cash on hand. Recognizing that, an alternative is to have an open line of credit available through a debt financier (likely a local or national bank with whom the practice has an existing relationship) that can be easily accessed in an emergency.

4. Practice emergency drills.

Depending on your age and from which part of the country you hail, many of you grew up with practice exercises for responding to simulated emergencies such as nuclear warfare, tornados, or fire. These practice exercises are a critical piece of preparedness. However, it is essential that organizations use "deliberate practice," which "involves attention, rehearsal, and repetition and leads to new knowledge or skills that can later be developed into more complex knowledge and skills."[6] This type of practice contrasts with rote repetition, which by itself will not improve performance. The benefits of deliberate practice include the following:[6]

- Increased likelihood of permanently remembering new information.
- Increased automaticity (applying knowledge automatically, without reflection).
- Increased ability to transfer practiced skills to new and more complex problems.
- Acquisition of subject matter expertise, thereby distinguishing novices from experts in a given subject.
- Enhanced motivation to learn more.

These benefits allow people to respond more quickly, more effectively, and more confidently in times of crisis.

Organizations can simulate actual events using unplanned emergency drills (where practical and appropriate, without causing unintended harm to patients or staff), plan in-service time to walk through a "dry run" of what actions to take in an emergency, or ideally, use a combination of both. The tabletop exercises should bring stakeholders together to walk through mock emergencies, with everyone acting out their role in the response. These activities often uncover gaps in the crisis action plan and, when completed routinely, help keep the plans "top-of-mind", so they are better remembered.

Deliberate practice should always be accompanied by ample guidance and followed with immediate and comprehensive feedback. Also, allow the training to build upon itself. Do not rush into an overwhelmingly complex simulation scenario before first developing some of the initial knowledge and skills (and confidence) that stakeholders will need to be successful; doing so could lead to frustration and an unwillingness to participate.

5. Test communication plans.

Communication plans should be routinely tested to ensure stakeholders receive critical information when they need it. Testing may include distributing automated test emails, automated test text messages, and automated phone calls. If the organization uses a phone tree as part of the overarching communication plan (often used by management teams within smaller medical groups), this should be tested as well. If the communication plan uses social media or an info@XYZ.com email address to receive and distribute messages, ensure the appropriate accounts and platforms are established, functional, and ready for use.

Within the testing process, audit the intended recipients to ensure they receive all test messages. If messages are not being received, determine the cause and provide additional education or change the program.

6. Safeguard documents.

Countless medical practices have lost vital paperwork in the regular course of business, ranging from the initial articles of incorporation to the current operating agreement to letters of non-renewability or certificates of need. Even physician employment agreements have gone missing as offices are moved or administrative leadership changes. It is easy to understand how records can be lost or destroyed during crisis times. Thus, a plan should be established for safeguarding critical documents. This may include physical security measures such as storage within a locked closet or a waterproof and fireproof safe, electronic archiving to avoid having to find an original paper document, or relocation to a secure, off-site location.

7. Plan with potential collaborators.

When a crisis hits, it often is reassuring to know you are not in it alone. One way to ensure your organization is not left flying solo in the face of a crisis is by forging relationships with peers during the pre-crisis planning stage. For medical practices, this could include creating a professional network with representatives from peer groups in your market who meet at least quarterly to discuss operational and strategic topics. At least once per year, network members should address crisis planning, with constituents sharing their own best practices and strengths, as well as an outline of their crisis plan. This provides an opportunity for all organizations to learn from each other's expertise and identify subject matter experts who are available for support in the event of an emergency. While these peer groups are often also seen as competitors within a given geographic market, there are many professional benefits to forming alliances. Take the time to build the relationships before you need the support.

8. Make your facilities safer.

In the aftermath of the 9/11 attacks, many facilities instituted new security measures to make them safer. Within healthcare settings, physical security should consider three key areas: access control, surveillance, and testing. Routine audits of physical security that assess these key areas are critical to identify areas that are vulnerable and need reinforcement and potentially detect any breaches that have already occurred. One example of an effective physical safety measure is badge access to clinical sites and critical support departments such as HR or finance.

9. Know evacuation routes.

Knowing how to safely exit a building from specific locations (as would be necessary in an active shooter situation) and vacate a geographic region (which could be essential with imminent flooding) is vital. In addition to displaying signage that clearly marks exits and evacuation routes, educate staff about evacuation routes and the protocols for evacuating patients and staff.

Many organizations publish guidance on evacuation procedures and even evacuation templates and checklists. (While hospital-specific, these can be adapted for use by medical practices, surgery centers, and other clinical spaces.) Examples of these resources include:

- Hospital Evacuation Checklist. Published by the California Hospital Association and accessible at www.calhospitalprepare. org/post/hospital-evacuation-checklist
- Hospital Evacuation Toolkit. Published by the Commonwealth of Massachusetts Department of Public Health and accessible at www.mass.gov/doc/evacuation-toolkit-planning-guide-0/ download
- Hospital Evacuation Plan Template. Published by the American College of Emergency Physicians and accessible at www.acep. org/globalassets/uploads/uploaded-files/acep/by-medical-focus/ disaster/hospital-evacuation-plan-template.doc

10. Assemble or update supplies.

Not every organization has ample space to keep excess inventory or supplies. Many medical practices operate on a "just-in-time" system, keeping necessary supplies on hand and replenishing the stock as needed. Thus, keeping supplies on hand "just in case" may seem like a luxury of space and dollars that cannot be afforded. However, even if it is a minimal supply, items such as personal protective equipment, bottled water, and batteries should always be readily available. The documented crisis plans should also include details about how to obtain additional supplies in an emergency.

11. Get involved in your community.

Many communities look to hospitals and medical groups as the single source of truth and often as a primary resource for support in the event of an emergency. In response, healthcare organizations must do their part to build connections with their communities. In many cases, this is a defined responsibility of the CEO, who manages the external relationships, supported by a COO, who manages internal functions. In the absence of a CEO, designate an individual who will consistently and positively act as your organization's "face." Encourage this person to participate in professional, faith-based, and/or civic organizations to carry messages to and from the community. Common examples include

Kiwanis, Rotary, and Lions clubs, and local affiliates of national health-care societies such as the American College of Healthcare Executives (ACHE), the Medical Group Management Association (MGMA), and Healthcare Financial Management Association (HFMA).

12. Document and insure the property.

It is essential to routinely inventory critical assets, document them with photos or videos, and detail their model numbers, purchase price, purchase date, and other relevant information. Then store the records in a secure place. Also, have the contact information readily available for the various insurance companies/agents, along with your policy number and filing instructions.

Chapter 12 details the insurance considerations relative to crises. For a quick review, FEMA publishes a summary document that outlines what various policies cover, accessible here: www.ready.gov/sites/default/files/2020-03/ready_document-and-insure-your-property.pdf.

In addition to FEMA's recommended 12 steps, a 13th is necessary for the healthcare industry: develop a plan to care for the caregivers.

A survey[7] completed at a recent Society for Health Care Strategy and Market Development (SHSMD) conference asked respondents to share their best tips on crisis responsiveness, including key lessons learned from those who recently experienced crises. Their aggregated input centered around three themes:

1. Plan and prepare.
2. Train and practice.
3. Take care of your team.

While the previous section highlights the first and second steps in the 12 steps outlined above, it is the necessity of the third theme that makes the healthcare industry unique in so many ways. With physician burnout at an all-time high, the importance of taking care of clinical, operational, and administrative support teams within healthcare delivery organizations is growing. In one example of day-to-day crisis management, Kaiser has begun rolling out a "purple scrubs" initiative. On every shift, one person who has mental health support training and is knowledgeable about available mental health resources wears purple scrubs, designating them as an accessible resource for anyone on the staff who may be in need.

If your organization does not have the internal resources to support your caregivers, consider educating staff on the availability of the Disaster Distress Helpline. This toll-free helpline provides crisis support services via telephone or text to those experiencing psychological distress resulting from man-made or natural disasters. It operates 24/7/365, is free, and has multilingual support. (To learn more, visit www.samhsa.gov/find-help/disaster-distress-helpline.)

Mental health support initiatives for caregivers are necessary every day and even more so during a crisis. Identifying care methods for the caregivers should be a crucial step in the overall crisis preparation process. Knowing how team members will be supported and sharing those methods in advance is extremely important in a field that has such a significant human element.

Again, reflecting on the work of Fischhoff et al.[3], the extensive preparations accomplished by completing each of these 13 key steps support completion of the third goal—changing behaviors. The intent is that this focus on preparedness will change how people think and ultimately act, so when the time comes and they need to spring into action, they are primed and ready to do so.

Prediction and Warning Systems

In support of the first of their 12 steps, FEMA publishes helpful information[8] on where to turn for alerts, warnings, and updates in times of crisis. These warning systems in the United States can be a resource at the onset and throughout the crisis. These include:

- Integrated Public Alert and Warning System (IPAWS): www.ready.gov/alerts.
- NOAA Weather Radio All Hazards (NWR): www.nws.noaa.gov/nwr
- Local Jurisdiction Emergency Notification Systems
  - Text and email alert systems: Conduct an Internet search of the word "alerts" along with your city or county name, or call or visit the website of your local public safety or emergency management office.
    - Enhanced Telephone Notification (ETN) systems: Check with your local emergency management team for further information and determine if this resource is available for your landlines, VOIP phones, and mobile phones.

— Outdoor sirens and/or voice alert systems: Check with your local emergency management team to determine if this service is still available in your community.

♦ Local school or organization notification systems: Systems can include notifications from workplaces, schools, communities, and faith-based organizations. Check with your affiliated groups to determine what resources they offer.

Many apps feature local alert functions. These include:
- FEMA: www.fema.gov/mobile-app
  — Learn more at www.fema.gov/mobile-app.
- American Red Cross: www.redcross.org/get-help/how-to-prepare-for-emergencies/mobile-apps.html
- The Weather Channel: www.weather.com/app
  — Learn more at www.weather.com/app.

For warning systems, FEMA summarizes the key actions for both individuals and organizations as follows:[9]

For Individuals

- Confirm your mobile device can receive wireless emergency alerts.
- Sign up for text and/or email alerts from your local jurisdiction.
- Consider purchasing a NOAA Weather Radio All Hazards.
- If you do not have a landline, check to see if your jurisdiction has options for VoIP and mobile phones connections to ETN systems such as Reverse 911©.
- Sign up for listservs and alerts for the workplace, schools, houses of worship, or other community organizations you will want to hear from in an emergency.
- Download relevant hazard alerts and warnings apps.
- Create a list of all the alert systems available to you and make sure everyone in the household receives the alerts as part of your household communication system.

For Organizations

- Test internal communication systems to ensure all individuals in the organization can be contacted.
- Designate individuals to be responsible for distributing alerts from official sources.

- Consider purchasing a NOAA Weather Radio All Hazards.
- List all the alert systems available for your community and your organization to guide people in the organization.
- Encourage individuals to sign up for alerts and warnings and assist them with finding any needed information.

Conclusions

In summary, the four critical areas of action identified by the National Academies (awareness, education, preparedness, and prediction and warning systems) are essential to mitigating the impact of a crisis. While distinct in function, they are a collectively robust set of tools to help organizations build their "good defense."

THE ROLE OF INCIDENT MANAGEMENT

Enabling a Rapid Response

Responding quickly to a crisis is one of the best ways to mitigate its downstream impacts. However, rapid response requires advance preparation, a coordinated team, and a systematic approach.

Recent research conducted relative to the effectiveness of rapid response teams in the healthcare delivery system concludes[9] that while a rapid response team functions well in managing patients in crisis or at significant risk, they are not without their challenges. These challenges include:

- Limited cohesion, driven by the inconsistency of team members.
- Limited opportunities to develop team skills or build relationships.
- Need for more advanced training than in traditional teams (those with consistent membership and less time-driven urgency to their work).
- Highly effective communication as a requisite to successful team performance.

While not all emergencies will be clinical emergencies, such as those faced by rapid response teams typically found within practices and hospitals, this study's learnings highlight several critical considerations that must be in place to enable a fast, effective response. These considerations include a dedicated crisis response team committed to working together and being available, consistent, engaged members of the group.

This team must undergo training to become familiar with their role and expected behaviors, learn about the other members of the team with whom they will be interacting (and their respective strengths and weaknesses), and develop the skills needed to function on an urgent or emergent basis.

Finally, rapid response will not be possible without seamless and complete communication to support it; the response team must be knowledgeable and communicative (see Chapter Four for further information regarding effective communication techniques.) To meet all these critical considerations, a systematic approach is necessary.

Incident Management Systems

Having a defined incident management system (IMS) is critical to the successful mitigation of a crisis. An IMS is "the combination of facilities, equipment, personnel, procedures, and communications operating within a common organizational structure, designed to aid in the management of resources during incidents."[10] According to the CDC, an IMS "reduces harm and saves lives,"[11] which speaks to its importance.

In 2004, the Department of Homeland Security developed and published information regarding the National Incident Management System (NIMS). NIMS "guides all levels of government, non-governmental organizations (NGO), and the private sector to work together to prevent, protect against, mitigate, respond to, and recover from incidents."[12] The intent was to create a plan that organizations could use, both alone and in concert with others, to manage various types of emergencies, from minor to catastrophic. While it is not a requirement for all healthcare organizations to follow NIMS, organizations must have an incident management system in place, even if it is one of their own developing.

NIMS' guidance[12] focuses on three major components and several subcategories:

1. Resource Management
   - Resource management preparedness
   - Resource management during an incident
   - Mutual aid

2. Command and Coordination
   - Tactical activities to apply resources on scene
   - Incident support, typically conducted at Emergency Operations Centers, through operational and strategic coordination, resource acquisition and information gathering, analysis, and sharing
   - Policy guidance and senior-level decision-making
   - Outreach and communication with the media and public to keep them informed about the incident.
3. Communications and Information Management
   - Supporting management in maintaining a constant flow of information during an incident by upholding the fundamental principles of:
     — Interoperability
     — Reliability, scalability, and portability
     — Resilience and redundancy
     — Security

The most recent version of the NIMS guidance provides 123 pages of details to support each of these items. Thus, even if your organization does not intend to follow NIMS plans, this publication is an excellent resource to use to build your own IMS and should be a vital tool for consideration during your pre-crisis planning processes.

Incident Command Systems

While all components of the NIMS plan are essential, the Incident Command System (ICS) and Emergency Operations Centers (EOC) addressed within the "Command and Coordination" component have applicability for most organizations and require a significant amount of prior planning to maximize their effectiveness.

ICS is the approach to on-scene incident management. ICS is the hierarchy of command; it helps ensure people from different departments or organizations can work together effectively and is one part of the broader IMS. While the ICS may vary depending on the emergency, a core structure should be in place for every incident. ICS is a vital part of pre-crisis planning and practice is important to ensure it works effectively.

The five major functional areas within the ICS are:

1. Command
2. Operations
3. Planning
4. Logistics
5. Finance/Administration

Concerning *command*, there are many types of incident commands, but for medical practices a single Incident Commander is likely sufficient. Figure 6.2 provides an example of the organizational structure of an ICS with a single Incident Commander.

FIGURE 6.2. ICS Structure with a Single Incident Commander[12]

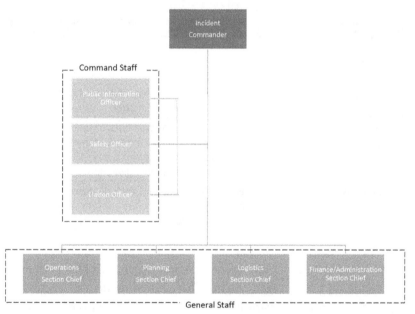

The other four functional areas support and are a critical part of the Command. Thus, it is critical to consider who will be part of each of the five functional areas and how resources can be assigned to ensure the person or people best able to assist in each area are the ones ultimately delegated to that area. Again, this speaks to the need to pre-plan, engage stakeholders in the planning process, and allow time to practice so the team members clearly understand their own role and how their work fits into the larger structure.

Emergency Operations Centers

The EOC is another vital component of incident management. The EOC is a location (a permanent physical facility, a temporary location, or a virtual space) where constituents can address the incident and coordinate support. One notable example of an EOC is that of the CDC. The CDC staffs an EOC 24/7/365 that is 24,000 square feet and has room for 230 people at one time. While the CDC's EOC is constantly functional, it varies in terms of its activation. The NIMS, which the CDC EOC uses, has created three activation levels, depending on the scale of the emergency at hand (see Figure 6.3).

FIGURE 6.3. EOC Activation Levels[12]

Activation Level	Description
3. Normal Operations/ Steady State	• Activities that are normal for the EOC when no incident or specific risk or hazard has been identified • Routine watch and warning activities if the EOC usually houses this function
2. Enhanced Steady-State/Partial Activation	• Certain EOC team members/organizations are activated to monitor a credible threat, risk, or hazard and/or to support the response to a new and potentially evolving incident
1. Full Activation	• EOC team is activated, including personnel from all assisting agencies, to support the response to a major incident or credible threat

Medical practices should define how and where their EOC will exist, depending on the emergency type. They should define the triggers for their activation at the various levels to ensure appropriate readiness within each activation level.

Importance of Informed Decision-Making

Research[13] by Kavan et al. contemplates the role of family physicians in managing patients in crisis. As part of their work, they developed an algorithm for effective crisis management, as seen in Figure 6.4.

While applicable as a stand-alone tool for physicians in family medicine or other specialties, the decision tree developed by Kavan et al. is an example of how to ensure timeliness and consistency in decision

FIGURE 6.4. Management of Patients Experiencing Crisis[13]

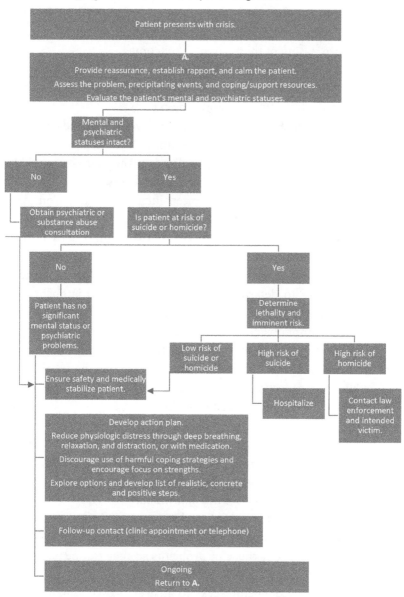

making during times of crisis. Also, it highlights the level of objectivity that is necessary when prescribing action to be taken during an emergency. Finally, it is one of the two most common tools used during the decision-support process.

Decision trees (used to support objective decision-making) and flow charts (used to support predictive sequencing) are essential during a crisis in that they identify potential consequences and help drive the thoughtful processing of these possible outcomes.

1. Decision Trees for Objective Decision-making
    - The Kavan algorithm is an example of a decision tree, which supports objective decision-making.
    - Decision trees are intended to be developed in advance of a disaster as part of pre-crisis planning.
    - However, they are operationalized in the management (also called mitigation) stage of the crisis process.
    - Decision-making trees are often included in the "Command Coordination" aspect of the IMS.
    - The decision on how to proceed follows in an orderly fashion, based on the premeditated rubric.
    - However, it is extremely important to note that using decision trees to determine action is only appropriate when the present circumstances are identical to, or very closely mirror, the assumptions under which the decision tree was developed. That is, if the present situation does not match the assumptions used to create the decision tree, it may be invalid as it does not reflect current realities or needs and thus should not be used to assist in decision-making.

2. Flow Charts for Predictive Sequencing
    - Flow charts, which support predictive sequencing, are developed (and most heavily utilized) in pre-crisis planning.
    - They are often a precursor to the development of the decision trees used for objective decision-making.
    - Akin to the "five whys" technique used in the Six Sigma DMAIC methodology, developing these types of charts helps identify the root cause of problems so they can be eliminated or prevented.
    - Predictive sequencing seeks to answer two key questions: "If this happens, then what happens?" and "What is the worst that can happen?"
    - Answering and documenting these two questions in advance allows one to develop a comprehensive picture showing how a crisis can unfold and ensures all possible outcomes (even those

with the slightest probability of happening or those that can occur only by chance) have been considered.

Just as Figure 6.4 provides an example of a decision tree that supports objective decision-making, Figure 6.5 is an example of a flow chart that supports predictive sequencing. It outlines the potential sequence of events resulting from a severe thunderstorm.

A range of possible outcomes from an intense thunderstorm are documented and their impacts defined in the flow chart. The flow chart allows for identifying potential issues an organization could realize when a thunderstorm hits, including disruptions in telecommunications systems, power outages, and fire. Informed about these possibilities, it is then possible for organizations to plan proactively for how they would address each issue.

Completing the process of predictive sequencing strives to prevent problems from occurring and to develop solutions that can be deployed quickly for the anticipated problems if they were to arise. This sequencing tool enables the most rapid possible response and the most informed decision making. The ICS can use decision trees to assist with all five critical areas, from Command to Logistics.

Crisis Communication Protocol

One of the most significant duties of leaders is their duty to inform. In simple terms, this duty requires leaders to meet three requirements:
1. Develop or identify information that users need,
2. Connect users with that information, and
3. Ensure messaging can be understood by users.[3]

Each of these requirements can be difficult to achieve for their own reasons during a crisis. For example, it may be difficult to develop information that users need when you yourself lack adequate information. The ability to connect users to relevant, accurate, and timely information is also of significance from a crisis mitigation perspective but can be difficult to achieve as stakeholders become dispersed or seemingly unreachable by telephone, email, or other traditional methods. Finally, trying to create a single set of messages that can be understood by both internal and external users is often impossible, requiring the development of differentiated communications for these two sets of users (and, as such, twice the time and effort).

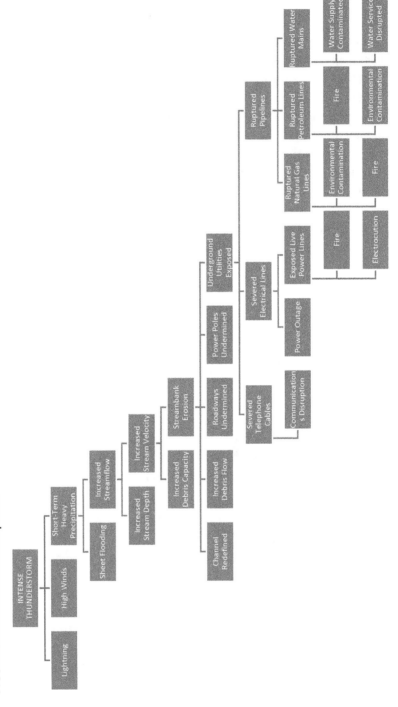

FIGURE 6.5. Natural Hazards Sequence[14]

Enabling leaders to meet their duty to inform amid a crisis is often not an easy task. However, the difficulty does highlight the need for crisis communication protocols, which streamline the process, drive efficiency of resources, and, most importantly, ensure stakeholders are informed about key events and actions required of them. As noted, an organization's IMS should ensure these communication protocols have been developed during the pre-crisis planning processes and are available for reference and use within the EOC. This allows the communication to follow standards, reflect the realities of the current situation, and ensure concordance with the organization's values.

While Chapter Four delves significantly into communication techniques during and after a crisis, we reiterate here that communication protocols must be in place, readily accessible, well understood, and practiced prior to the onset for crisis for them to ultimately be effective when they are most needed.

SUMMARY

Much of the ability to mitigate a crisis lies in the preparations that occur before the crisis exists. However, organizations must sufficiently expand their concept of "preparation" to ensure they are completing all necessary tasks. This includes the need to increase awareness of the potential and probability of crisis, education regarding the types of crisis that may be most impactful to a particular organization, taking actions to prepare (guided by a multi-step process), and being aware of the harbingers of danger to come. This work, coupled with rapid responsiveness, informed decision-making and effective crisis communications, will allow a crisis to be best mitigated.

RESOURCES

1. National Academies of Sciences, Engineering, and Medicine. *Strengthening the Disaster Resilience of the Academic Biomedical Research Community: Protecting the Nation's Investment.* Washington, DC: The National Academies Press; 2017. https://doi.org/10.17226/24827. Accessed April 2, 2021.
2. Dyrda L. The 5 Most Significant Cyberattacks In Healthcare For 2020, Monday, December 14th, 2020. Becker's Hospital Review. www.beckershospitalreview.com/cybersecurity/the-5-most-significant-cyberattacks-in-healthcare-for-2020.html. Accessed April 2, 2021.

3. Fischhoff B, Brewer N, Downs J, eds. Communicating Risks and Benefits: An Evidence-Based User's Guide." US Department of Health and Human Services, Food and Drug Administration; 2018. www.fda.gov/about-fda/reports/communicating-risks-and-benefits-evidence-based-users-guide. Accessed April 2, 2021.

4. FEMA. Hazard Info Sheets. www.ready.gov/sites/default/files/2021-01/ready_full-suite_hazard-info-sheets.pdf. Accessed April 2, 2021.

5. FEMA. 12 Ways to Prepare. www.ready.gov/sites/default/files/2020-11/ready_12-ways-to-prepare_postcard.pdf. Accessed April 5, 2021.

6. Brabeck M, Jeffrey J, Fry S. Practice for Knowledge Acquisition (Not Drill and Kill). American Psychological Association. Teachers' Module. 2010. www.apa.org/education/k12/practice-acquisition#:~:text=Practice%20is%20important%20for%20teaching,information%20(Anderson%2C%202008).&text=When%20students%20practice%20solving%20problems,new%20and%20more%20complex%20problems. Accessed April 5, 2021.

7. SHSMD. Health System Command Centers and Their Impact on People, Process, and Platform. Resource Digest. www.shsmd.org/resources/crisis-communications-hospitals-and-health-systems-shsmd-resource-digest. Accessed April 5, 2021.

8. FEMA. Know Your Alerts and Warnings. /www.ready.gov/sites/default/files/2020-03/ready_know-your-alerts-and-warnings.pdf. Accessed April 5, 2021.

9. Leach LS, Mayo AM. Rapid Response Teams: Qualitative Analysis of Their Effectiveness. *American Journal of Critical Care*. 22(3):198–210. https://doi.org/10.4037/ajcc2013990. https://pubmed.ncbi.nlm.nih.gov/23635929/. Accessed April 5, 2021.

10. Ready.gov. Incident Management. www.ready.gov/incident-management (February 17, 2021) Accessed April 5, 2021.

11. CDC. CDC Emergency Operations Center: How an EOC Works: A Model for Response. September 18, 2020. www.cdc.gov/cpr/eoc/how-eoc-works.htm. Accessed April 5, 2021.

12. FEMA. National Incident Management System, Third Edition. Washington, DC: FEMA; 2017. www.fema.gov/sites/default/files/2020-07/fema_nims_doctrine-2017.pdf. Accessed April 5, 2021.

13. Kavan MG, Guck TP, Barone E J. A Practical Guide To Crisis Management. *American Family Physician*. 74(7):1159–1164. www.aafp.org/afp/2006/1001/p1159.html. Accessed April 5, 2021.

14. National Research Council. A Safer Future: Reducing the Impacts of Natural Disasters. Washington, DC: The National Academies Press; 1991. https://doi.org/10.17226/1840. Accessed April 5, 2021.

CHAPTER 7

Financial and Economic Issues

Benjamin Franklin once said, "By failing to prepare, you are preparing to fail." Nothing could be more accurate for the development of a financial strategy as it relates to crisis management. A reliable, pre-developed financial plan is key to weathering any crisis. This chapter outlines the basic financial process that any organization should have in place so they can "weather the storm." Although planning does not guarantee that the crisis will not be painful, it might ensure that the business remains viable throughout the situation.

DO NOT WAIT UNTIL A CRISIS TO PREPARE

The first admonition relating to a financial strategy is "Don't wait." Foresight is critical. A well-run business will look ahead at the potential issues on the horizon and plan accordingly; the potential for crises is one of them. If an organization waits until it is in a crisis, it will be in "reactive" mode versus being proactive. Reactivity will inevitably put more strain on an organization. First, it will require much more energy. During a crisis, the organization's leaders need to be able to deal with the problem at hand. If a solid financial plan is already in place, the organization can focus on other vital matters rather than finance. Second, it will likely cost less, which means that in a reactive mood, one tends to "throw money" at problems to make them go away. Spending money without much forethought will likely result in the consumption of more economic resources in a time when money may be scarce. Because focus and financial resources will be in short supply amid a crisis, pre-planning will ensure that these valuable resources are well invested in dealing with the situation.

LIQUIDITY

Liquidity is crucial. As defined by Investopedia, *"Liquidity refers to the ease with which an asset, or security, can be converted into ready cash without affecting its market price."* Stated another way, "Cash is king." During a crisis, having liquid assets will provide significant financial security. Whether in cash or assets that can readily convert to cash, this liquidity will allow the organization to pay its financial obligations even if revenue begins to dry up.

Liquidity was a key consideration with many medical groups during the COVID-19 pandemic. As the economy quickly came to a halt, many medical groups were no longer able to generate revenue by seeing patients. Unfortunately, operational expenses are still incurred despite income drying up. This matter created much consternation for medical groups, resulting in one or all the following actions:

- Laying off/furloughing staff
- Borrowing money
- Capital calls from owners
- Not paying bills
- Bankruptcy
- Being forced to sell the entity to another organization

None of the above positions are desirable and can have a lasting (negative) impact on the organization. For example, borrowing money can create a financial hole that may take years to repay. The same is true for furloughs/layoffs. If those staff members have been long-time employees and function in "knowledge positions," they may not be available for rehire when the organization reaches that point. The cost to recruit or re-train staff is real and can have a long-term impact on practice productivity.

So, liquidity is critical.

Organizations gauge their liquidity by several primary industry ratios. The two basics are the current ratio and the quick ratio. The equations for these two ratios are:

$$\text{Current Ratio} = \text{Current Assets} / \text{Current Liabilities}$$

$$\text{Quick Ratio} = \text{Cash} + \text{Short Term Investments} + \text{Accounts Receivable} / \text{Current Liabilities}$$

The denominators of the two ratios are the same, but the numerator is different. The critical difference is in the definition. The Quick Ratio is looking at assets that can quickly convert to cash. The Current Ratio looks at assets that can reasonably convert to cash within a year. So, while both are important to ensure proper liquidity, the Current Ratio could be considered as a mid-term liquidity ratio for a business like a medical group. In contrast, the Quick Ratio could be an excellent indication of short-term liquidity.

Both are important and require monitoring. Having healthy ratios will indicate that liquid assets are available if a crisis were to strike. Unfortunately, the idea of maintaining strong liquidity ratios runs counter to many medical groups' methods. Many medical groups keep limited cash on hand (the primary source of liquidity), paying out as much as possible and as frequently as possible to the owner physicians in the form of compensation. Tax implications could result from keeping much cash on hand, depending on the entity's legal structure and other factors; balancing these competing dynamics is critical.

Another essential consideration for liquidity is understanding an organization's fixed versus variable costs and the overall flexibility in its cost structure. If an organization's revenue suddenly decreased, would much of its expense structure follow, or would the expense structure remain mostly unchanged? The former would infer a primarily variable cost structure, while the former would infer a predominantly fixed cost structure. A variable cost structure is most advantageous during a crisis in that it is easy to reduce expenses as revenue falls; however, outside of an emergency, the more an organization can leverage costs (meaning, drive higher revenue using the same cost structure), the more profitable it can become.

Moving to a completely variable cost structure does not make sense, as it infers only short-term thinking and/or assuming the worst-case scenario will inevitably occur. However, having a solid understanding of how an organization's costs will change with revenue and working to find the right balance of fixed vs. variable costs for your organization will help to ensure liquidity in a crisis.

ONGOING MONITORING

In discussing financial management and crises, the previous section outlines some key considerations relative to preparation and liquidity. An action that goes hand in hand with these concepts is based on the idea of having dependable ongoing monitoring of financial performance. It is not easy to have a financial plan and maintain reliable finances if you are not regularly monitoring what is going on financially inside your organization. Smaller organizations tend to have limited monthly financial reporting.

The following actions are beneficial to ensure the ongoing financial health of your organization will enable it to weather a financial crisis:

- **Monthly financial reporting:** Using your organization's financial reporting tool (QuickBooks, for example), a balance sheet and income statement should be prepared each month. These reports should not just be put into a drawer but should be reviewed in detail.
- **Variance analyses:** Use the monthly financial reports to identify variances from month-to-month and year-to-year. If expenses are creeping up with no corollary change in revenue, implement a remediation plan.
- **Ratio analyses:** As outlined above, consider the various ratios, such as the Current Ratio and the Quick Ratio Also include Days in Accounts Receivable (AR), Profit before Provider Compensation as a percent of Professional Collections, comparisons to relevant industry data, and others.
- **Bank statement reconciliations:** Bank statements should be reviewed and reconciled regularly.
- **Comparisons of the practice management system to the accounting system:** Comparisons and reconciliation of these two systems' data should occur regularly to ensure that they are trending alongside each other. Although timing differences may cause some variance, they should be limited.

Highlighted above are *some* of the actions that should occur regularly within an organization. There are likely others that are specific to organizations, but this sets the "minimum baseline." Ensuring a solid and ongoing understanding of an organization's finances will give it the ability to pivot quickly to respond to a crisis.

BE PREPARED TO MAKE THE TOUGH DECISIONS

Crises are *problems*, and survival is critical. To ensure that the organization can weather the storm financially, its leaders may have to make tough decisions.

Generally, the organization should be prepared to make these tough decisions, but the timing is critical. The organization should try to avoid "jumping the gun" and choosing a course of action too early; it may not be necessary. At the same time, if the organization waits too long, it may be too late; the organization may be too far gone for the tough decisions to have an impact on their financial viability.

Additionally, a plan to outline the tough decisions should occur well in advance of having to make them. For example, the organization should develop several different "playbooks" for distinct scenarios, depending on the severity of the crisis. That way, "game time" decisions are not being made on the spot. Only those that are well thought through in advance are being executed.

With respect to these decisions, financially, the organization should look to make cuts where there is an intersection between the maximum financial benefit to the organization and the least amount of impact for the organization to sustain its operations and generate revenue. Obviously, these are competing forces, but identifying where they intersect is vital. In many cases, the decisions will revolve around personnel cuts. The focus should be on those who are not "mission critical" to the organization. Given the organization's relationships with many of these individuals, the tendency will be to see them *all* as mission critical. The goal will be to make certain loyalties are aligned—first to the viability of the organization and then to the people within the organization. A lack of clarity on this point could sink the organization.

While deciding upon which individuals are mission critical, it will also be necessary to define criteria. Meaning, will a salary reduction preclude a full furlough? Is a more permanent reduction in force needed? Options and the pros/cons should be weighed in the balance. For example, an overall salary reduction may equal permanently eliminating two staff members. Although there may not be a "right" or a "wrong" decision here, the implications could be lingering. For example, while an overall pay cuts may keep the staff gainfully employed and viewed as a shared sacrifice, it may be demoralizing to certain employees, especially if much of the weight of responding to the crisis is falling on their shoulders. So, it is vital to weigh decisions carefully. There is no right answer.

Another key consideration concerning making tough decisions is being willing to make sacrifices yourself. It may be energizing to an organization's culture if the leadership makes the same or greater sacrifices than those asked of the other employees. This is a true sign of leadership—that the organization's leaders will be "first in line" to take the hit out of deference to the organization and its employees. Sacrificing is not easy, as the leaders will feel much of the pain and will likely be working double-time to react/respond. If it were, everyone would be doing it!

REVENUE STABILITY

In the context of proactivity, organizations can take steps to ensure that their business model is almost crisis proof. One of these approaches is looking at revenue streams and identifying ways to create revenue stability. While there are several tactics to do this, three primary methods are outstanding.

First, make sure your revenue streams are tied to a commodity that will be needed regardless of a crisis. The more an organization can ensure that the services they sell will be in demand continuously, the less impact they will feel from a crisis. An example of this would be the difference between cosmetic plastic surgery services and primary care services. In a crisis situation, individuals will quickly forego cosmetic plastic surgery but will still demand primary care services.

Even within a specialty such as primary care, another way to ensure revenue stability is to consider the services tied to the pricing model. Examples of this are concierge services and capitation arrangements. With both concierge services and capitation, less of a primary care physician's revenue is tied to fee for service than to subscription-based, and it is received regardless of whether services are delivered. This arrangement provides much more insulation than a fee-for-service model. In a fee-for-service model, if patients' ability to access care is turned off in an FFS model, the revenue spigot is turned off; however, the spigot keeps running in these alternative payment models, creating much more stability.

The final revenue stability factor we will consider is the method of delivering the services. The recent COVID-19 pandemic highlighted the phenomenon of telemedicine. Historically, the reliance on telemedicine has been very low, with most patients preferring in-person visits. Once the ability to schedule in-person visits ceased, the ability to generate revenue diminished as well. Those organizations that were equipped to deliver care via telemedicine modalities still had the ability to generate revenue, allowing for a more stable revenue base.

In summary, consideration of the type of services, the type of revenue streams tied to those services, and the method of delivering those services can impact revenue stability. In turn, revenue stability can create a more solid financial platform that will allow an organization to weather a crisis.

INSURANCE IS IMPORTANT

Insurance becomes essential amid crises and can help to protect against the financial implications of the situation. There are many different types of insurance. These can include, but are not limited to, the following:

- General Liability
- Auto
- Health
- Life
- Disability
- Worker's Compensation
- Key Man (Life)
- Professional Liability
- Errors and Omissions
- Cyber
- Earthquake
- Flood
- Kidnap and Ransom
- Reputational Risk
- Umbrella

Insurance hedges risk. You pay a small sum of money on an ongoing basis to protect against the unlikely event that a crisis will occur requiring a much larger financial outlay. By concept, the more likely an emergency is to occur, the more costly the insurance will be. Thus, organizations must make solid financial decisions about what types of insurance make sense for that organization. The basis of decisions can depend on 1) the cost of the insurance and 2) the likelihood of an event occurring that that type of insurance covers. For example, using a rather extreme example, kidnap and ransom insurance is likely not needed for most medical groups in the United States, but could very well be a necessity in other parts of the world. Similarly, it may be worth considering key man insurance, but depending on the age and health of the "key man," it may not make financial sense to take out a key-man policy.

Organizations should work closely with their insurance brokers to assess their respective organization and associated risks to make sure that they are adequately covered in the unlikely event of a crisis. A review of insurance coverage should occur at least annually. Further, the organization should understand for what they are and are not covered and use the insurance when the need arises. It does not make sense to pay for insurance but not use it when the policy would otherwise be activated.

TAP INTO RESOURCES

Depending on the type of crisis in play, there may be other sources of financial relief, especially with events like hurricanes and floods where specific governmental relief programs are available. Relief is also obtainable for infrequent occurrences, such as the COVID-19 pandemic. As a result of the significant financial strain on businesses, the government enacted various forms of relief that organizations can access. Consultation with an organization's accounting and legal representatives is vital in determining the risk/reward of tapping into these resources. (See Chapter 11, Legal and Regulatory Hurdles.) As an example, the Paycheck Protection Program came with a few "strings" attached and legal complexities that require some level of expertise to navigate. While the program may be very beneficial to an organization, it is critical to understand all aspects of the program before participating.

BE AN OPPORTUNIST

As a final financial word of this chapter, organizations that do well to execute on the above can take advantage of unique opportunities amid a crisis. If other organizations are suffering financially and your organization is healthy, that creates opportunities. These can include but are not necessarily limited to:

- Acquire other businesses at a discount
- Offer employment to top talent that their current employer has let go
- Purchase property at a discount
- Negotiate favorable contracts
- Create more goodwill with current employees by offering strong incentives during a crisis

Having a solid financial plan does not only allow an organization to survive during a crisis, but it can enable the organization to thrive. This is the position an organization wants to be in!

SUMMARY

Solid financial planning is key to weathering a crisis. The steps outlined in this chapter are not to infer that an organization will be crisis-proof, financially, but they should help ensure that an organization can make it through a crisis. the objective is to thrive vs. merely survive.

CHAPTER 8

Operational Crises

Crises can impact any and every area of operations for medical groups and provider organizations. Considering the broad array of crises that influence operations, it is impossible to prepare for every unique scenario. Instead, focus on developing and communicating several key action plans that can be implemented in response to various crises and adjusted as necessary for each circumstance. It is more important to create a condensed *playbook* that all employees and providers know well than a response plan for every possible scenario or crisis. In some cases, you may implement multiple crisis response plans.

Clear communication and proactive preparation are critical to any operational area, and those tenets apply to managing operational crises. Crises that vary significantly in origin can have similar impacts on operations. For example, a regulatory turmoil and a global pandemic could both negatively impact patient volume and revenue in diverse ways, but they will require some similar responsive actions. This chapter will examine several types of crises and discuss operational response plans and preparation that could apply to various scenarios.

FINANCIAL

Many crises negatively affect business operations, but some financial crises can permanently alter the fundamental economics. There is a saying in the business world that goes, "No margin, no mission." Many organizations are highly dependent on a few key revenue drivers that are critical to profitability.

For any business, it is essential to acknowledge critical elements and proactively plan for disruptors. We tend to take capstone services and products for granted, putting blinders on to anything that would change the economic paradigm. A new technology, shifting consumer/patient preferences, and competitive landscape changes appear to evolve overnight, and you want to be as prepared as possible. Blockbuster, Kodak, and AOL are classic examples of lack of innovation and/or refusal to acknowledge change that can become deadly.

Leaders often can predict financial crises if they have the time and talent to focus on strategic development. There are scenarios, however, in which a financial crisis could not have been predicted, and damage control was the only option. In all situations, a proactive approach is recommended to identify potential weaknesses, implement operational adjustments, and reduce or avoid negative financial impact.

Below are several tactics to mitigate and manage financial crises:

1. **Research.** Gather information from relevant sources on an ongoing basis. Read pertinent news and stay up to date on developments that affect your industry, market, and specific services.

2. **Protect the Vital Signs.** Identify the critical services and pillars that are essential to sustaining the business. Without these services and revenue streams, the business will not exist. Prioritize these services at the highest level and communicate constantly with key stakeholders to improve, adapt, and grow these components of your business.

3. **Innovate.** Acknowledge the need for change and constantly identify ways to improve operational processes, enhance revenue, expand services, and better manage expenses.

4. **Prepare for Worst-Case Scenarios.** If the economics of the business change tomorrow, what are your minimal operational thresholds to stay in business? Determine which services and resources could be suspended or removed to keep the business economically viable.

A financial crisis is often the result of other issues that may have been developing for an extended period. A healthy amount of anxiety and scrutiny can help avert financial disaster, but when that is not sufficient, be prepared with a *bomb shelter* plan that may save the business.

PERSONNEL

Personnel crises can often be a repercussion of unrelated events such as the workforce shortage related to COVID-19 that has caused ongoing staffing and employment issues. Personnel falls into many classifications requiring a wide variety of circumstances to manage. Employed physicians typically have a unique perspective compared to employed medical assistants or receptionists, and good leaders will acknowledge those differences and address them as needed.

In all personnel matters, an objective approach with consistent communication is recommended. Physician burnout, union tension, disgruntled employees, and general morale issues can all be considered personnel crises that are detrimental to your business. Consider the following to help manage and lead a successful operation in the face of such headwinds:

- **Proactively Communicate.** Address issues promptly rather than waiting for them to boil over; do not be afraid to have the tough conversations. Generally, all personnel will respect and appreciate hearing tough messages rather than being left in the dark.
- **Develop Mentors and Champions.** Leadership can be lonely, so build a team in addition to formal leadership roles to help manage challenging issues.
- **Manage Personally and Objectively.** Set clear guidelines and establish systems of accountability, empowering other leaders as well.
- **Establish Goals.** Communicate objectives regularly and tie daily activities and outcomes to organizational strategy and success. Celebrate successes and acknowledge failures.
- **Cultivate Respect.** Build a culture that demonstrates commitment to people and purpose. Everyone plays a role in the organization's success. Be willing to part ways with a *high performer* to preserve this culture.

POLITICAL AND REGULATORY FACTORS

A political and/or regulatory crisis can have highly variable effects on different businesses due to multiple factors such as location, patient demographics, payer mix/relationships, and political relationships. These crises often lead to other crises discussed in this chapter, particularly the economic repercussions that can result from a change in political office or covered services.

We have experienced several political and regulatory changes in 2020 that have or will impact business operations in healthcare.

Insurance coverage for telehealth services was a necessary adjustment that will likely forever shift the fundamental delivery of healthcare. Mandatory wage increases and suspension of elective services are other examples that have compounding effects on business operations that may lead to other forms of crises.

For some organizations, politics and operating budgets go hand in hand where local propositions and political matters affect healthcare organizations' funding. A local vote or election could lead to a financial crisis if political matters are not managed effectively.

The challenge with these crises or developments is to react without panic and on time. Many leaders want to jump into action or apply the quick bandage when it is often more effective to wait until a more informed decision can be made to adjust operations adequately. However, the challenge is not to wait too long, realizing that complete information may never be available to allow organizations to be fully confident in critical decisions.

Recommendations to manage political and regulatory crises:

- **Stay Current.** Read and stay up to date on local and national political developments that could affect your business. Significant changes do not usually happen overnight.
- **Develop Strategic Relationships.** Partnerships could help identify and/or protect potential disruptors to your business. Fierce competitors may rally together for the collective good in response to certain crises.
- **Establish a Compliance Plan.** Implement a comprehensive plan and actively manage it. Many organizations prioritize compliance too low and are at risk for any number of disruptors that could damage operations. Stay current and seek input as needed. Because accountability is crucial, develop checks and balances to keep your organization and leaders engaged. It is much better to audit internally before a third party does an audit.

IMMEDIATE SAFETY

Crises involving immediate safety cannot be ignored in today's world. We will not attempt to cover all the concerns and variables here, but these crises could be active shooters, natural disasters, fires, or inclement weather. While some of these may seem unlikely, it is still important to be prepared; we truly never know when the all-too-common angry patient could escalate to create a volatile situation.

The Occupational Safety and Health Administration (OSHA) requires a written Emergency Action Plan (EAP) "to facilitate and organize employer and employee actions during workplace emergencies." OSHA has developed a checklist available at www.osha.gov/SLTC/etools/evacuation/eap.html to address general issues, evacuation policy and procedures, reporting emergencies and alerting employees, and employee training and drills.

The challenge operationally is to keep this information fresh and ensure continuity through personnel turnover and potential changes. Incorporate this into annual training programs and communicate consistently, leveraging current events to prompt conversation and reminders for your organization.

CULTURAL AND PUBLIC UNREST

Cultural movements and developments have had a significant impact on business operations throughout history and particularly in recent years. More recently, businesses have been forced to adjust operations or close entirely because of COVID-19 repercussions, Black Lives Matter protests, political strife, and other demonstrations of civil unrest.

Preparing in advance is a challenge because these crises often develop quickly and without warning. They also manifest differently in specific markets or regions, making it challenging to balance the appropriate level of response or forecast direct implications for your operation. Communication is most critical both internally and externally with customers, patients, and key stakeholders. We have all experienced under and over communication from businesses during these scenarios; *balance* is the key.

- **Communicate Responsibly.** Identify key audiences and group them by level of detail or frequency of communication. Employees may require more frequent and detailed communication than patients or customers.
- **Rely on Leadership.** Trust talented leaders to make good decisions. If you do not have strong leadership, then proactively

address that as a separate issue. Crisis scenarios often highlight weak leadership, but that is not when you want to be made aware.

- **Be Willing to Change Direction.** These situations evolve rapidly, and it may not make sense to hold on to your first position or response forever.
- **Stay Informed and Objective.** As a leader, put the organization first and captain the ship through the storm. Trust your intuition, but listen to your employees, patients, and partners. Like any good captain, rely on and leverage the talent around you to achieve the best outcomes.

Leaders often feel pressure to have the answers and respond quickly to comfort or assuage concern, which is often impossible and/or not the most effective approach. Be willing to take a breath and communicate that you are still gathering information. You can be responsive and communicate effectively without providing answers or a definitive plan. Your response to cultural and public crises will likely require collective wisdom and leadership to manage effectively.

STRATEGIC AND COMPETITIVE

Strategic or competitive crises manifest in many ways, and, in healthcare, every market (defined broadly) has unique circumstances to manage. A shortage of primary care providers could limit the ability to provide care to an underserved market, and then a nearby city may be oversaturated with primary care due to large competitive systems' network development strategy. Payer dynamics and value-based care could further influence these strategies. The comprehensive impact to your market and organization may be driven by layers of strategy deployed at a national level and then filtering down.

These crises are the ones that keep operators up at night, and well they should. Competition is fierce and becoming more so as healthcare borders are removed, national networks are developed, large health systems grow, and telehealth services expand target markets. A *friendly* health system or practice could align or be acquired by a larger entity with a more threatening strategy, which happens all the time in markets across the country. Healthcare investors' influence is also driving new competitive strategies focused more on financial return than quality and delivery of healthcare services.

The best defense is a good offense. Do not sit and worry about what *could* happen, but proactively develop and implement strategies that you can or want to control. Set a clear vision for the organization, communicating regularly about how every person contributes to the pursuit of that vision, and execute operationally with follow-through and accountability. Competition is only becoming more complex with the nationalization of healthcare, price transparency, modern technologies, and shifting reimbursement.

SUMMARY

Without a crystal ball or magic mirror, it is impossible to see everything coming. Still, by employing some of the tactics and basic concepts we have discussed in this chapter, you will be better prepared to manage a crisis of any nature. Your organization is already in a better place with leaders who take the initiative to read books like this and proactively plan for the future. Proactive preparation and communication will help you make the optimal objective decisions with the help of your team.

CHAPTER 9

Cybersecurity and Crisis Management

Until recently, cyber threats were problems for larger organizations and something most of us read or heard about in the news. However, after years of attack, these larger organizations have spent millions of dollars fortifying their IT infrastructure, making medical practices and hospitals the new soft targets for cyber criminals. Until now, cybersecurity awareness and prevention has been the information technology (IT) department's worry; now, the attacks are so debilitating that cybersecurity has become an organization-wide crisis management issue.

For healthcare organizations, Cybersecurity brings with it significant compliance stipulations. For example, the Health Insurance Portability and Accountability Act (HIPAA) security rule requires that healthcare entities covered by HIPAA conduct a security risk analysis (SRA) of their organization. Non-compliance can result in harsh penalties.

In this chapter, we address cybersecurity breaches, sources of threats, the chief information officer's (CIO) responsibilities, working with third-party vendors, and conducting privacy and security risk analyses. The information will help your organization take proactive steps to gain ground in developing and maintaining a healthy cybersecurity posture. There is much catching up to do.

CYBERSECURITY BREACHES ON THE RISE

Healthcare cybersecurity is a growing concern, as evidenced by the steady rise in hacking and IT security incidents in recent years. Many healthcare organizations have struggled to defend their network perimeter and hold cybercriminals at bay. Now, more than ever, healthcare providers must protect multiple connected medical and non-medical devices. Additionally, the number of Internet of Things (IoT) devices that are integrated into the healthcare industry has exploded. Data is the new currency, and cybercriminals will stop at nothing to gain access to this valuable commodity. These offenders are developing more sophisticated methods to attack healthcare organizations and increase their chances to cash in this data by holding it ransom or selling it on the black market.

The 2019 HIMSS Cybersecurity Survey[1] provides valuable insight into U.S. healthcare organizations' information security experiences and practices. Polling of more than 160 U.S.-based health information security professionals revealed:

- **A pattern of cybersecurity threats and experiences is discernable across U.S. healthcare organizations.** Significant security incidents are nearly universal in U.S. healthcare organizations, with many of the events initiated by bad actors leveraging email to compromise their target's integrity.
- **Healthcare cybersecurity practices are advancing.** Healthcare organizations appear to be allocating more of their information technology budgets to cybersecurity.
- **Complacency with cybersecurity practices can put cybersecurity programs at risk.** Certain responses are not necessarily bad cybersecurity practices but may be an early warning signal about potential complacency seeping into the organization's information security practices.
- **Notable cybersecurity gaps exist in critical areas of the healthcare ecosystem.** The lack of phishing tests in some organizations and the pervasiveness of legacy systems raise serious concerns regarding the healthcare ecosystem's vulnerability.

External Attacks

More large healthcare data breaches were reported in 2020 than in any other year since the HITECH Act called for the U.S. Department of Health and Human Services' Office for Civil Rights to start publishing healthcare data breach figures on its website.

In 2020, healthcare data breaches of 500 or more records were reported at a rate of more than 1.76 per day. 2020 saw 642 large data breaches reported by healthcare providers, health plans, healthcare clearing houses and business associates of those entities – 25% more than 2019, which was also a record-breaking year.

More than twice the number of data breaches are now being reported than 6 years ago and three times the number of data breaches that occurred in 2010.[2]

FIGURE 9.1. HIMSS 2019 Cybersecurity Survey

Recent Significant Security Incident	2019					2018
	Hospital	Non-Acute	Vendor	Other	Total	Total
Yes	82%	64%	68%	76%	74%	76%
No	14%	33%	30%	20%	22%	21%
Don't Know	4%	3%	3%	4%	4%	3%

Source: HIMSS 2019 Cybersecurity Survey[1]

Unfortunately, many healthcare organizations have been slow to respond to cybersecurity threats and generally lag other industries in prevention. Cybersecurity budgets are increasing, and healthcare entities purchase new cybersecurity technologies, yet healthcare entities still struggle to thwart attacks and keep their networks secure proactively.

Insider Threats

In addition to cybersecurity attacks from external actors, healthcare organizations continue to deal with challenges inside their organizations. Securing healthcare data and managing an effective cybersecurity program can be daunting. According to a recent Verizon Data Breach Investigation Report, 58% of healthcare PHI breaches are by insiders.[3] The report states that healthcare is the only industry where internal actors are the greatest threat.

Healthcare data are primarily used internally and are shared with individuals to facilitate the coordination and delivery of care. Coordinating and delivering care is complicated in and of itself; securing the data while ensuring access to those who need it adds a layer of complexity. Despite the transition to electronic health record (EHR) systems, paper records are causing data security problems, according to the Verizon study. Hard copy documents were the assets most often involved in incidents entailing error.

Healthcare organizations, therefore, should consider instituting an effective risk management program that invests in comprehensive data breach detection. This program would include table-top exercises and reviewing Internet of Things (IoT) security as just a few prevention and detection requisites. Additionally, healthcare leaders must ensure that internal staff has adequate cybersecurity training and resources to guarantee the appropriate precautions to protect sensitive data from compromise by internal and external bad actors.

CYBERSECURITY AND TODAY'S HEALTHCARE CIO

Among other regulatory compliance requirements, cybersecurity continues to be top-of-mind for healthcare chief information officers (CIOs), chief information security officers (CISOs), executives, and boards. Healthcare entities continually face the challenge of balancing secure, protected health and financial information with providing authorized access within and across the organization, including external entities. As CIOs seek ways to achieve this delicate balance, they are trying to move from a reactive to a *proactive* position in several key areas, including the following:

1. **Network Perimeter Security.** Also known as a demilitarized zone (DMZ), perimeter security addresses the boundary between the private, locally managed, and owned side of a network and the public and externally managed network such as the Internet. The DMZ is one of the highest security risks and must be assessed, tested, and addressed continually.

2. **EHR System Security.** This includes attention to passwords, audit trails, dual authentication, role-based security profiles.

3. **End-User Authentication.** We have seen a continual rise in the number of legitimate users logging on to an organization's wired or wireless network to access protected health information. This escalation increases the amount of network traffic to monitor for unauthorized access. CIOs need assurance that all log-in attempts are monitored and acted upon accordingly. Some CIOs have implemented a single-sign-on (SSO) solution to control and resolve these issues. Whatever solution the organization deploys, it must test, document, and resolve authentication issues continually.

4. **User Identity.** More organizations are implementing a virtual desktop infrastructure (VDI) in their EHR environments. It often becomes difficult to capture and audit user identities in these environments, which further raises security risks.

5. **Internet-of-Things (IOT).** An exponential number of devices are becoming computer-based and linked to the Internet. IoT apparatuses such as biomedical, security cameras, and HVAC systems must be identified, continually monitored for security risks, and managed.

Merely complying with privacy, security, and confidentiality regulations is no longer sufficient. Violating these regulations often results in tens or hundreds of thousands of dollars in fines, not to mention potential destruction of an organization's information assets, an adverse patient outcome, or negative publicity. CIOs must secure and monitor their networks, applications systems, and data while conducting periodic security audits.

As the number and complexity of IT systems, devices, and users increases, forward-thinking CIOs welcome third-party advisors to conduct ongoing security audits, assessments, and penetration tests using human interaction with specialized automated tools. The existence of and compliance with updated privacy and security policies are under closer scrutiny, so organizations must offer employees cybercrime and security education and training on an ongoing basis.

CIOs are **expected** to develop and implement a cyber defense strategy to protect their healthcare organizations and patient information. Those CIOs who openly assess their vulnerabilities, prioritize their actions, and continually monitor and manage their security risks are in the best position to help their organizations grow efficiently, effectively, and safely.

THIRD-PARTY VENDORS

As if dealing with your own security threats was not challenging enough, you must also ensure all your business associate (BA) partners are compliant. (A business associate is a person or entity, other than a member of the workforce of a covered entity, who performs functions or activities on behalf of, or provides certain services to, a covered entity that involves access by the business associate to protected health information.)

Many organizations mistakenly assume a signed business associate agreement (BAA)is sufficient for ensuring that third-party vendors are compliant and responsible for their breaches. (Covered entities must ensure that they have a current HIPAA business associate agreement in place with each of their partners to maintain PHI security and overall HIPAA compliance. These partnerships are known as business associate agreements BAAs.)

While having a BAA is a critical first step, it is not enough. There are three common misconceptions about the BAA:

1. The third-party vendor or person doing work for the hospital/ practice is not storing PHI data and therefore they are not considered a BAA. This presumption is *false*. If the vendor has access to data, they qualify as a BA and must sign a BAA.

2. All third-party vendors use encryption and offer a privacy statement. Again, *false*. They still have access to the data and encryption is not always a 100% safeguard.

3. The vendor has a BAA with the hospital and practice; any subcontractors or partners are under the same BAA. **False**. As soon as PHI is entered in the vendor's system, they are automatically deemed a business associate. Further, *any* subcontractors working on behalf of the vendor or the practice are also considered business associates. The latest rules state that covered entities MUST obtain satisfactory assurances from their business associates no matter how far down the chain the information flows. Everyone involved needs to be under a BAA, and it is your responsibility to make sure they are.

Many security breaches happen because primary vendors use unidentified, down-the-chain resources who are not directly contracted with the hospital/practice. In some cases, these are individuals who are from staffing agencies and/or work as freelancers and are unaware of policies or standards. They carry no insurance and have no means of protecting anyone if they cause a breach, so there would be little to no recourse. Further, they may not even be in the United States. These strategies can reduce the possibility of security threats when working with third-party vendors:

- All subcontractors must be preapproved. Under no circumstances can any vendor use subcontractors without prior permission.

- Vendors must disclose all existing subcontractors and require each to sign the BAA provided by the hospital/practice and present proof of insurance. If covered under the primary vendor's insurance policy, evidence is required.
- All vendor contracts should require provisions about cybersecurity breaches. Specifically, the vendor must be responsible for their mistakes and for the cost to remediate the issue.
- The BAA should have a breach notification requirement mandating the vendor to notify of any incidents.
- There should be a data return policy and/or destruction requirement.
- System access should have a start and end date. Most systems today allow for setting an expiration date.
- The right to audit and inspect adherence to these policies at any time should be required.
- Vendors must provide evidence of their security risk analysis, compliance certifications, and staff privacy training.
- Policies and the BAA should be revisited after each major upgrade, new release, and version change, as new contractors are often introduced during these events.
- Consider adopting contract management software to help manage and track key dates and documents as these BAAs are updated annually.

RESPONDING TO A BREACH/INCIDENT

Responding to a cybersecurity breach/incident can be alarming. These ordeals are challenging to manage because the criminals often are invisible and unstoppable once they control a network. In some cases, you do not learn about the incident for months or even years later. In other cases, the criminals launch a brute force attack and disable a network or conduct a ransomware attack, demanding money to return the data. In any event, here are some short- and long-term responses to consider:

During an Attack
- Immediately disconnect the entire network from the internet to block any other access and data transfers.
- Quarantine all infected devices. These will be needed for the investigation.

- Determine who has been infected or impacted. An example may be everyone who clicks on the suspicious link/email. It is critical that NO one is punished for making a mistake; otherwise, people may conceal their mistakes out of fear of losing their jobs. This information is crucial to properly respond, so **do not** make anyone feel uncomfortable for coming forward.
- Immediately loop in all vendors and IT staff so they can start their investigation.
- Bring in counsel familiar with cybersecurity regulations and incident response protocols. From this point forward, all communication **must** go through counsel; otherwise, you can forfeit your client/attorney privilege. Counsel will help you determine if you need to call in the authorities, notify patients, contract the media, and provide additional guidance.
- Conduct a comprehensive investigation and document *everything.* Start pulling together all your policies and network diagrams as the investigators will need this information.
- Contact your cybersecurity insurance agent; they likely will have their experts join the investigation.
- *Do not assume this is a breach.* In most cases, these incidents are not actual breaches. You will have 60 days to investigate before you are required to respond based on the findings. (If you can reasonably show there was not a breach, the incident does not require a report to the ONC.)

After the Attack

- Depending on the type of breach and the circumstances, you may need to self-report. Each incident is different, so it would not be possible (or appropriate) to provide specific recommendations. Moreover, these guidelines do change, so we recommend following the official HHS/HIPAA official website for guidance on responding to a breach. Access the appropriate information at www.hhs. gov/hipaa/for-professionals/breach-notification/index.html

THE IMPACT ON COVERED ENTITIES

Organizations that maintain thorough and well-documented HIPAA compliance and risk management programs reduce their risk of financial exposure to civil monetary penalties from HHS/OCR. Preserving the appropriate privacy and security documentation necessary to satisfy compliance with key HIPAA security rules is critical. This also includes conducting a security risk analysis (SRA) to help covered entities avoid the fourth and highest-level of liability: "willful neglect—not corrected." The SRA should be performed at least annually and include assessing the covered entity's technology infrastructure and information security policies and procedures. The SRA should consist of a remediation plan to outline the actions to address any weaknesses in the organization's security program.

The use of risk analysis and risk management tools, such as the ones leveraged by Coker Group, can be significant resources in assessing and managing any gaps identified through the SRA process. Risk analysis tools can provide a method of documenting each recognized risk event or vulnerability point in the organization, including those with business associates. They also serve as a repository of your organization's security remediation efforts and evidence in the event the covered entity is subject to an audit from the Office of Civil Rights (OCR). This detailed documentation validates that a covered entity has an effective risk management program and may help prevent the "not corrected" status associated with the $1.5 million annual limit.

Also, OCR has stated that it will be actively auditing organizations that *do not* report any breaches. Therefore, covered entities with the most accurate security risk analysis and comprehensive breach detection program will reduce the likelihood of the imposition of fines and penalties because of a security audit or breach.

SUMMARY

The 2019 HIMSS Cybersecurity Survey findings suggest that healthcare organizations' cybersecurity initiatives are moving in the right direction with some degree of uniformity. However, we still have a long way to go in comparison to other industries. While the progress is positive, budgets allocated to cybersecurity are still inadequate to deal with all the emerging cybersecurity threats that most healthcare organizations face. Moreover, the lack of knowledgeable cybersecurity personnel also continues as a detriment to progress.

Legacy systems and lack of staff awareness continue to present a problem in need of innovative approaches. Overall, healthcare organizations are moving in the right direction, but bad actors continue to stay one step ahead in the game.

Coker Group and its partners have developed a comprehensive and cost-effective approach to conducting a risk analysis that meets the nine essential elements required by The Office of Civil Rights (OCR). For additional information on Coker's comprehensive cybersecurity risk analysis, contact us at 800.345.5829 or email info@cokergroup.com.

RESOURCES

1. HIMSS. 2019 HIMSS Cybersecurity Survey. www.himss.org/sites/hde/files/d7/u132196/2019_HIMSS_Cybersecurity_Survey_Final_Report.pdf. Accessed October 30, 2020.
2. 2020 Healthcare Data Breach Report: 25% Increases in Breaches in 2020. Posted By HIPAA Journal on Jan 19, 2021. www.hipaajournal.com/2020-healthcare-data-breach-report-us/. Accessed June 7, 2021.
3. Snell E. 58% of Healthcare PHI Data Breaches Caused by Insiders. Health IT Security. March 5, 2018. https://healthitsecurity.com/news/58-of-healthcare-phi-data-breaches-caused-by-insiders. Accessed October 30, 2020.

CHAPTER 10

Personnel Considerations

Every type of crisis will bring about some degree of personnel and behavioral change across the breadth of your organization. Consequently, it is important to anticipate these potential changes and have a plan to meet the challenges. This chapter focuses on some of the human resources considerations that may arise during a crisis, including the overall makeup of the staff, their roles and responsibilities, dealing with them from a regulatory and legal standpoint, and other personnel-related issues. We also include ways to address employees' tension, stress, and other mental health issues.

Crisis response can be costly to an organization from both a financial and personnel standpoint. Healthcare organizations of every size and composition must be ready for a crisis to the degree possible with a well-thought-out crisis "playbook."

General George S. Patton said, "Prepare for the unknown by studying how others in the past have coped with the unforeseeable and the unpredictable." This sentiment is particularly significant regarding planning for a crisis.

CRISIS MANAGEMENT PLANNING TEAM

Every organization should have a crisis management team in place, comprised of a cross section of individuals who know how the organization operates. The group should be diverse and include representatives from each functional area, such as clinical, finance, facility operations and maintenance, office administration, front end/patient processing, information technology and electronic health records, and possibly others. Committee members' expertise about what makes the organization run efficiently during non-crisis times will provide the critical insight to ensure operations continue during and after a crisis. If the organization's business operations must be modified, these experts will know what changes the organization can make and still produce acceptable outcomes. They will know if some non-critical parts of the organization can be suspended temporarily and the personnel performing those tasks can be redeployed in other, more critical areas of the organization that must be kept running.

Jonathan Raymond, author of *Good Authority: How to Become the Leader Your Team Is Waiting For* said, "You can't know what you don't know. You can't know about things you have yet to discover." The crisis management planning team needs to encompass those who *do* know everything about how the operation functions—those who can use this knowledge to consider all the aspects of business continuity.

STAFF CONSIDERATIONS AND PLANNING DECISIONS

When a crisis affects business operations, the organization must determine whether staff members can continue to perform their standard roles or whether some must be laid off or redeployed. The representative from the human resources department can advise on those decisions and their implications.

As part of the crisis management planning process, as noted above, consideration needs to be given to the critical elements of the organization's operations and what aspects must continue during the crisis. If some areas of operations are unnecessary for a time, can those employees be redeployed to perform other functions in the organization? A crisis team leader or captain in each department should recommend to the planning team which employees should be reassigned to what other function. Here are some matters to consider:

- Determine training requirements for employees who are redeployed to perform other functions in the organization. Who will deliver that training?
- If an employee is not needed during the crisis and cannot be redeployed, the employee's employment status must be considered. Options might include furloughs, leaves of absence, or terminations. Usually, senior management and the head of human resources make these decisions with input from legal counsel.
- If the organization's building has been damaged or destroyed, can employees work from another facility or from home? If working remotely, is the technology in place and set up (hardware and

software) so they can be productive? (Ensure the proper cybersecurity precautions are in position to protect the organization from any type of data breach or other vulnerability.)

A communication plan will need to be developed for informing the employees about any personnel changes and addressing their questions. For example, if employees are furloughed, how long will it last? How will their pay be affected? What about benefits, vacation pay, and paid time off? If terminations are necessary, questions may revolve around medical and other benefits, termination or severance pay, and eligibility for rehire. Depending on the number of employees affected, terminations may trigger the Worker Adjustment and Retraining Notification Act (WARN), including notice obligations for the organization. Your legal counsel or human resources representative can provide advice.

REGULATORY AND LEGAL CONSIDERATIONS WHEN DEALING WITH STAFF

Providing a safe and healthy working environment is a fundamental responsibility of the organization's leadership that must continue during and after a crisis.

Some of these provisos may include working conditions, transportation or parking accommodations, climate control, and personal safety equipment if needed on the job. The organization should have clear safety protocols, such as appointing fire captains responsible for fire safety regulations and evacuation procedures. Fire drills should be held regularly with evacuation procedures posted in conspicuous places.

During and after a crisis, additional regulatory and legal considerations may come into play, depending on the crisis' scope and nature. For example, in planning for a possible health crisis such as a pandemic, the organization should consider the following measures to ensure a safe and healthy environment:

- Providing personal protective equipment (PPE) such as masks, gloves, and other safety or sanitation equipment.
- Having hand sanitizer stations throughout the workplace, with sanitizing protocols for staff, patients, and visitors to follow.
- Placing social distancing markers on the floor to keep staff, patients, and visitors six feet apart.

- Putting elevator protocols in place to limit the number of employees using the elevator at a time to prevent close contact.

It is crucial to consider, in advance, how additional legal and regulatory requirements around local, state, and federal requirements may affect employees. If a reduction in force (RIF), furloughs, or job reassignments are planned, certain legal requirements may need to be addressed in advance of these actions. The senior human resources professional and legal counsel should be involved in these personnel decisions to ensure matters go as smoothly as possible once the employees learn of the changes.

Issues to consider when planning furloughs and terminations include:
- Who will decide which employees will be affected by potential terminations or furloughs?
- What adverse impact might the actions have on a group based on age, race, sex, or other protected classes?
- Who will deliver the news to the affected employee(s)? Develop a script or talking points to verify that the communication is clear and consistent to all employees.

Anticipate questions that will come from affected employees and prepare for those question in advance.

Here are a few examples to consider:
- Will a severance plan be offered? If so, what will each employee receive? Who will deliver the specifics to each employee?
- Is a signed release form required to receive the severance pay? If so, what is the deadline for signing and returning it?
- Are terminated employees eligible for rehire when business improves?
- If the action is a furlough, how long will it last? Will the employees on furlough be able to keep their medical or other benefits? If so, for how long, and if not, how soon will they be ended?
- What COBRA benefits options are employees eligible for and what is the cost?

Most of these questions will need to be answered by human resources, with possible input from legal counsel and the organization's medical insurance broker or provider. If employees have additional

questions, the human resources representative should be readily available and easily accessible to handle them.

The rest of the staff must be informed, as soon as possible, about the terminations and/or furloughs. The most senior leader often delivers this communication in person if the employees are in a central location; if employees are in remote locations or cannot meet in person, a video or phone conference call is an option. Explaining the purpose of the action with empathy, sincerity, and straightforward communication is recommended, followed by written communication that outlines these details. All employees must receive the same information so there is no misunderstanding.

If an employee is injured or dies during a crisis, the organization has additional procedures to follow, including contacting the employee's emergency contact/next of kin, local authorities, insurance providers, and OSHA (if applicable). Workers' Compensation reports may also need to be completed and filed. The human resources representative and legal counsel should take the lead in this process, using the established company guidelines and procedures. If the news media and the community's level of interest is high, take extra care in handling any communication. Thinking through multiple crisis scenarios in advance and considering the proper protocols to follow in each situation are effective ways to be prepared.

Other Related Personnel Issues

Dissension

Dissension among employees is common during times of crisis and may manifest itself quickly due to heightened uncertainty, stress, or unwanted change. Dissent is usually the result of an emotional reaction to an event or series of events. Most people do not show dissent unless they feel strongly about something. It may be unrelated to work but might still result in negative attitudes or behaviors that affect the employee's productivity and team members.

There are several ways to address an employee's dissent during a crisis. Potential actions include:

- Show concern by actively listening to the employee, encouraging them to be open about their feelings, and asking what is disturbing them.

- Depending on the situation and nature of the disagreement, provide justification or an explanation for the issue that is causing the dissent. Sometimes nothing will satisfy their concern (such as returning to their work location after a fire or flood until the building is fully repaired and passes building inspections). However, explaining the situation and the reasons immediate solutions are not available may put them back on a more even emotional keel.
- If possible and prudent, address the cause for the dissent.

Listening, explaining, and, if possible, addressing the situation, may resolve the dissent from that employee and potentially others with similar concerns. This reaction also shows that the organization's leadership understands and is empathetic to the employee's concerns and pro-active in addressing their discontent during the crisis.

Stress and Tension

Employees must be aware of good mental health practices and employers must be supportive and offer resources that will promote good mental health. During and after a crisis, it is even more important that employees and employers be on alert for possible mental health problems and provide ways to maintain good mental health.

Mental health problems have their roots in a variety of areas and can be exacerbated during a crisis. For example, some people may feel overly stressed by the changes that the crisis caused them relative to their work situation, which may generate poor mental health. Those who suddenly must work from home may feel isolated and miss daily contact with their colleagues. Others may be afraid of losing their job and the subsequent financial issues.

Mental health issues may manifest themselves in anger, irritation, depression, or sadness. The employee may lack motivation and have trouble concentrating. They may feel tired, burned out, and overwhelmed at work.

These mental health issues can affect the employee's health and affect their performance, as can lifestyle factors such as lack of quality sleep, poor diet, lack of exercise, and drug or alcohol use. These issues can harm work performance and, if not addressed and treated, can develop into more serious long-term health problems.

All these issues are treatable, and employers can offer a variety of options to assist in this effort. Employees should be aware of the impor-

tance of caring for their own mental health and reminded of things they can do to stay mentally healthy. These include:

- Cultivating and sustaining their personal social life, including doing activities with friends and family and participating in non-work events with other people.
- Asking peers for support and reciprocating to keep each other mentally strong.
- Creating time on their schedule for calming or relaxing activities that promote positive mental health, such as yoga, meditation, or walks.
- Participating in physical activities.
- Developing healthy eating habits.

Other mental health improvement activities, such as group meditation or virtual yoga classes during lunch breaks or after work, can promote team camaraderie and positive mental health. Resiliency and stress management classes may be valuable as well. Local, state, and national organizations also provide free mental health resources to organizations and their employees.

Morale-boosting activities can be easily organized and implemented among employees, including video, voice, or email messages from the organization's leaders. Company-wide updates or town hall meetings by Zoom or video conference in which senior leaders give updates and answer questions from employees can be uplifting.

Fun social activities could include trivia night, virtual team happy hours, name that tune contests, or other entertaining social activities that allow employees to de-stress and build positive mental health during stressful times.

Additionally, the employer may provide outside resources such as mental health clinics and therapists through the company's medical insurance plan. Many employers offer an Employee Assistance Program (EAP), an outside provider organization that gives employees confidential access to trained professionals who can help them address various issues such as substance abuse, financial problems, relationship discord, or other mental health concerns.

Employers can also provide wellness opportunities to their staff at work by encouraging short breaks on the job, offering flexible scheduling to meet employee work-life balance requirements such as family

and childcare needs, and sending regular emails regarding maintaining positive mental health and well-being. It is also essential to encourage and promote to employees the importance of caring for their own mental health and offering ideas such as those above.

Many employers also offer proactive ways to promote positive mental health in the workplace, especially during the recent 2020 COVID-19 pandemic, when millions of people suddenly found themselves working remotely. Being away from their business location and colleagues can increase feelings of isolation and confinement, which elevates stress levels—an additional mental health challenge.

Some individuals handle stress and isolation better than others, and managers should know how each employee is faring. For example, single parents and parents with young children may have additional challenges. Having homeschooling responsibilities while working from home may present additional stress and challenges. Managers should be attentive to their employees' stress levels and check in with them regularly to see how they are doing and to find out if there is anything they can do to make the work situation as positive as possible, such as flexible work arrangements that meet both the organization's needs and the needs of the employee and manager. Improved technology, including video conferencing, makes it easier to accomplish workarounds than it was just a few years ago. These considerations also can help employees feel more connected and less isolated, which can improve their mental health.

SUMMARY

With proper planning that considers the impact of the crisis on the staff, as well as regulatory and legal matters, organizations can be better prepared to manage the myriad issues that may arise during and after the event.

Organizations should develop a playbook that addresses many of these concerns and use it as a resource during the crisis. Although you will never be 100% prepared to handle every detail that will affect employees during a crisis, with proper planning and foresight, you can have a blueprint to follow to be more successful in handling these matters during a disaster and in its aftermath.

CHAPTER 11

Legal and Regulatory Response When a Crisis Occurs

During the past several decades, organizations throughout the world have been affected by significant crises such as natural disasters, pandemics, supply chain interruptions, and environmental disasters. These massive events have impacted organizations' financial well-being.

Fortunately, many organizations have effective crisis management plans in place and are committed to dynamic planning processes to promote continued business operations. However, as attorney James Haggerty points out in his blog Provoke (provokemedia.com), "All crises are legal crises," and "legal issues are inexorably intertwined with the actual physical event at the heart of what is typically considered a 'crisis'." Legal counsel plays a critical role in crisis planning, which involves balancing legal risk and preservation of organizational reputation.

CRISIS DEFINED

One definition of crisis that resonates is as follows: A crisis is an event perceived key stakeholders to be "highly salient, unexpected, and potentially disruptive" and recognized as having four key characteristics: (1) sources of disruption, uncertainty, and change; (2) threatening or causing harm to organizations and their stakeholders; (3) a behavioral occurrence, meaning recognized as being "socially constructed by the actors involved rather than a function of the depersonalized factors of an objective environment"; and (4) components of larger processes rather than isolated events.[1]

The Institute of Public Relations states that in addition to financial loss, public safety, and reputational threats, other industrial accidents, and product harm can result in injuries and even loss of lives. Crises can create financial loss by disrupting operations, creating a loss of market share/purchase intentions, or spawning lawsuits related to the crisis.

The Association of Corporate Counsel polled its members in 2011 reported that in the previous five years, 64% of them had faced some type of corporate crisis. The most frequently occurring types of crises experienced by the responders were compliance-related (19%), natural disasters (16%), tort/accident, workplace (i.e., employee misconduct, harassment, violence) (each 11.2%), and environmental crises.

Due to the frequency and potential impact of crises on healthcare organizations, an effective crisis management plan is essential.

CRISIS MANAGEMENT FROM A LEGAL PERSPECTIVE

To be effective, crisis management must address the most significant threats first. The immediate concern in a crisis must be to maintain the safety of the public. Failure to do so magnifies the harm associated with the crisis. Only after public safety has been addressed can financial and reputational threats be tackled. The goal of crisis management is to protect organizations from the identified threats and/or to lessen the outcome associated with the threat.

Additionally, crisis management requires a multi-phasic approach to be effective and can be divided into three phases: pre-crisis planning, crisis response, and post-crisis evaluation and response. Prevention and preparation are the crux of the pre-crisis planning phase. In the crisis response phase, leadership must execute and respond to the crisis. Finally, post-crisis response involves critically evaluating the crisis response and using lessons learned, building improvements into the crisis response plan.[1]

Pre-Crisis Planning

Preparedness planning experts believe organizational damage can be mitigated by developing an effective plan for responding to critical incidents. Best practices for such a proactive plan include a crisis management plan and incident response team that is established, trained, and has practiced their response prior to an incident occurring; a centralized command center or decision-making body; "dry runs" of the crisis plan; and importantly, the engagement of legal counsel throughout each of the crisis management plan stages.

It is imperative to involve legal counsel early, as an attorney provides key support to organizations developing response plans for the variety of crises that can arise. During a crisis, public relations concerns, communications planning needs, legal strategy formulation, and many other processes and actions must function in concert. With the many threats crises pose to an organization, legal counsel plays a vital role in aiding the organization in not only analyzing the threats but helping leaders understand and balance the various risks associated with different courses of action.

A best practice named by an Association of Corporal Counsel poll was the recommendation that the crisis management plan effectively reduce the number of potential crisis scenarios included in the plan and, instead, zero in on the most important risks that the organization should protect against. According to ACC's Crisis Management and the Role of In-house Lawyers: Company Leading Practices, "You're never going to be able to completely document everything that might happen within a company, nor should you try to do so; such a plan would be voluminous and impractical. There will be key areas of risk that a company's legal department knows will be relevant given the in-depth corporate knowledge an in-house legal team has with respect to the company it serves; these are the types or incidents a plan should focus on."[2] Additionally, maintain flexibility. The interplay of dynamics during a crisis require adaptability of the entire team.

Risk Assessment and Training

Understanding risks and vulnerability associated with such risks permits an organization to expend valuable resources on those areas that hold the greatest threat potential. Performance of routine risk assessments and the associated business impact analysis is crucial to the development of the crisis management plan and enables an organization to focus on key risks as set out above. Equally important is using the information obtained from these exercises to train key individuals and employees. Training should be catalogued and records kept demonstrating the ongoing, cyclical nature of this process.

A comprehensive strategic crisis management plan is imperative for an organization to navigate successfully through a crisis. Doing so positions an organization in preserving its reputation and stakeholder confidence.

Crisis Response

As addressed in earlier chapters, having in place a crisis response team that is poised to spring into action immediately based upon the established crisis management plan is essential. Ensuring the crisis response team is cross-functional is an important matter not to overlook, including ensuring legal counsel and risk management are included.

Communication Response

An organization's communication response is one of its most important actions during and after a crisis. Involving organizational counsel early will ensure the messaging mitigates or averts a negative outcome. Counsel also can make certain communications are developed in advance, are consistent with organizational policies, and appropriately balance the risks and interests of the organization.

Best practices for an effective, timely communications plan include:
1. **Ensure that public safety is the priority.** Attempt to have the initial response communicated within the first hour.
2. **Carefully check all facts to ensure accuracy.** Particularly with response times of within one hour, the potential for inaccurate information can be high.
3. **Be consistent.** Ensure intra-communications are high so that all key spokespersons are communicating the same message.
4. **Identify and use all communication avenues, including mass notifications, internet, intranet, and social media.**
5. **Express and communicate sympathy for victims, where applicable.**
6. **Be sure employees receive the initial response as well.**
7. **Where applicable, prepare to provide trauma counseling to affected individuals, including employees and their families.**[3]

Legal Counsel's Role in a Crisis

The importance of legal counsel's role in navigating a crisis cannot be understated. Healthcare organizations are fortunate to have compliance and risk departments that are fully participative in many regulatory and risk response processes. However, in some situations that arise during a crisis, without a counsel's involvement, legal risks may go unidentified and unaddressed.

Anticipating the need to communicate with regulators is an essential component of a well-thought-out plan. Legal counsels' role in such communications is significant. Counsel who have previously established relationships with regulators may have an advantage during times of crisis because such a relationship can ease discussions on the content of press releases before they are circulated. A best practice identified by the ACC poll was including template regulatory notice drafting as part of the pre-crisis planning process.

Multi-State Practice Issues

During the COVID-19 crisis, the Centers for Medicare & Medicaid Services (CMS) and other payers relaxed telehealth requirements and many providers began increasing their use of telehealth to ensure uninterrupted access to care. One consideration in telehealth is the state's rules and regulations with respect to licensure of a provider providing telehealth services to a patient in a different state. Each state has its own framework and must be researched and analyzed to remain in compliance.

Newly Issued Regulations and Governmental Guidance/Waivers

As laws, regulations, and other guidance are issued, they must be reviewed, interpreted, and applied according to the nature of the crisis. Failure to involve legal counsel in such interpretation could result in a misunderstanding of not only what is permitted, but also what is required, thus increasing the overall risk.

Area-Specific Expertise

Addressing legal issues in a crisis does not diminish the importance of area-specific expertise. Examples include patient privacy and security regulations, personnel/human resources issues, emergency credentialing, as well as general crisis response. Legal input will likely require coordination across risk, compliance, legal, and outside advisors.

Scope of Practice and Credentialing Issues

The issue of credentialing out-of-state healthcare providers is a relevant consideration during the crisis response phase as augmentation of the workforce may be necessary depending on the circumstances. In certain situations, this may mean expanding the number of available care providers; in other instances, expanding the types of care these individuals deliver may be necessary. Additionally, volunteer healthcare providers and those coming out of retirement to assist may need special support to encourage their participation.

Seventy percent of approximately 10,000 volunteers polled in 2006 indicated that the potential exposure to liability was a critical factor in their deciding to assist in an emergency. Solid legal protections for these individuals means wider availability of essential healthcare personnel during crisis events where an expanded workforce is needed.[1]

Certain laws in various states temporarily allow existing healthcare providers to work beyond the boundaries of their traditional expertise. Pharmacists may be asked to administer vaccinations, nurses may be asked to function at a higher level and permitted to deliver care as nurse practitioners, and emergency medical technicians may be permitted to dispense prescriptions. Still other states permit retired healthcare providers to provide a limited scope of services on a temporary basis, such as palliative care, consistent with their training and expertise.

An interstate organization, the Uniform Law Commission, is advancing an agenda for interstate credentialing by drafting the Uniform Emergency Volunteer Health Practitioners Act, which any state can adopt. It includes provisions for interstate recognition of healthcare licenses to address credentialing of healthcare providers across states. Although the scope of practice for a given provider is limited for out-of-state healthcare providers, the act goes a long way in facilitating effective disaster-response. The law, in draft form, attempts to remove this key barrier to expanding the workforce during times of crisis while also promoting interstate cooperation.

EMTALA

The Emergency Medical Treatment and Labor Act (EMTALA) enacted in 1986, requires hospitals to provide emergency care to all patients, regardless of their ability to pay. Failure to comply with the EMTALA regulations is a significant concern for hospitals because not only a hospital experience fines and penalties, but they can also be excluded from participating in the Medicare program.

The law affects the ability of emergency departments to respond in a disaster because hospitals must first perform a medical screening exam to determine if an emergency medical condition exists. The medical screening exam might require certain labs and other imaging exams to make the emergency medical condition determination. And, if an emergency medical condition in fact exists, the hospital must stabilize the condition prior to transfer. During a crisis response situation, triaging patients to alternate care sites can be the difference between life and death for some patients.

Meeting the EMTALA requirements butts up against practical considerations for efficiently and effectively responding to the emergency; however, when the secretary of Health and Human Services declares a public health emergency and the president declares an emergency or a disaster pursuant to the National Emergencies Act or the Stafford Act, Health and Human Services can issue a "1135 waiver" that temporarily suspends sanctions for noncompliance with certain provisions under both HIPAA and EMTALA.[5] These waivers have been enacted in the past, including during the COVID-19 pandemic, and can be put in place quickly (and retroactively) during a disaster setting.

HIPAA

The Health Insurance Portability and Accountability Act (HIPAA) is another key law that must be considered during a state of emergency. HIPAA provides a framework of privacy protection of an individual's health information. One can imagine the stressors imposed on communications when a disaster or mass casualty incident strikes. As discussed above, waivers may be issued by HHS under certain circumstances, but not always. However, not all emergencies will appreciate a reprieve from compliance with federal law. Where no HIPAA waiver is available, a clear understanding of a covered entity's obligations is imperative to avoid liability and potential penalties arising from noncompliance.

It is important to remember, however, that HIPAA has certain provisions that assist covered entities in responding to emergencies, even where no waiver has been issued. These provisions permit disclosure to law enforcement to identify individuals, to public health agencies, and to disaster assistance organizations. There is also a degree of flexibility built into HIPAA in terms of disclosure of information for treatment, payment, and operations. Care coordination falls within the permissible disclosure of patient information and certainly application of care coordination in a broader approach than routinely considered may be necessary.

In addition to treatment purposes, HIPAA permits the following even without a waiver.

Public health activities: An organization can disclose patient information without an authorization to a public health authority, to a foreign government at the direction of a U.S. public health authority, and to people at risk of contracting or spreading a disease, if permitted by state law.

Disclosures to family, friends, or others involved in patient care. An organization can share patient information with a patient's family, friends, or other people identified by the patient as involved in his or her care. Information about a patient can also be disclosed to identify, locate, and notify family members or anyone else responsible for an individual's care. This information is limited to the patient's location, general condition, or death.

Disclosures to prevent an imminent threat. An organization may share patient information to prevent or lessen a serious and imminent threat to the health and safety of an individual or the public at large. This provision permits a covered entity to disclose a patient's information without an authorization to anyone who can prevent or lessen the threatened harm.

Disclosures to media or others not involved in patient care. An organization is permitted to provide facility directory information to acknowledge whether someone is a patient and to provide general information about the patient's condition. This is the case only if a patient has not otherwise objected to being included in the facility directory.

Minimum necessary rule. As always, any information disclosed about a patient must be limited to the "minimum necessary" to accomplish the purpose. Covered entities must be aware of state privacy laws. Where the state privacy law is stricter than HIPAA, the state privacy law must be adhered to. This is another area where involvement of counsel is imperative.[5]

SUMMARY

Addressing crisis is a cross-functional effort. Highly functioning organizations understand the necessity of involving legal counsel in all stages of crisis management. This includes planning, response, and debriefing. Despite what legal rules are in place, the legal landscape will be continuously shifting during an emergency, and all organizations will likely have to adjust their response accordingly. The interplay of the various laws and regulations requires thoughtful analysis and practical application to navigate through a crisis situation.

REFERENCES

1. Bundy J, Pfarrer MD, Short, CE, et al. Crisis and Crisis Management: Integration, Interpretation, and Research Development. *Journal of Management.* 46(6):1661–1692.
2. Association of Corporate Counsel. Crisis Management and the Role of In-House Lawyers: Leveraging Cross-Functional Expertise. Leading Practices Profile Series. Washington, DC: Association of Corporate Counsel; 2016.
3. Institute for Public Relations. Crisis Management and Communications White Paper. October 2007. https://instituteforpr.org/crisis-management-and-communications.
4. Bundy J, Pfarrer MD, Short, CE, et al. Crisis and Crisis Management: Integration, Interpretation, and Research Development. *Journal of Management*, 46(6): 1661, page 11. -5. Ibid., page 12
5. Institute for Public Relations, Crisis Management and Communications White Paper. October 2007, https://instituteforpr.org/crisis-management-and-communications.
6. FindLaw (2018) 42 U.S.C. § 1395dd - U.S. Code - Unannotated Title 42. The Public Health and Welfare § 1395dd. Examination and treatment for emergency medical conditions and women in labor.

CHAPTER 12

Insurance Considerations

A s crises occur, viable insurance products provide opportunities to mitigate financial losses. These products can address the economic losses and help mitigate the emotional and psychological stress that crises present. In this chapter, we consider various opportunities to soften the financial blow for the organization experiencing a crisis.

Like all insurances, the coverage terms and conditions should be carefully reviewed to ensure that when a crisis arises and an insurance claim is considered, the insurer will agree that the coverage is applicable and the payments are appropriate.

OVERVIEW: CLAIMS THAT RESULT FROM INSURANCE POLICIES

Working in healthcare has its risks, but many exposures can be abated through insurance products. Though expensive, insurance may be a useful tool to offset emotional, psychological, and economic concerns. While some insurance products are difficult to tie directly to specific situations, many allow the owner to have some peace of mind that the insurance reimbursement will lessen or cover the economic loss or exposure.

Business Owners' Policies

Most healthcare businesses carry a package of insurance policies covering a broad array of potential liabilities and losses that result from crises and other claims-related situations. Often, the solution is a master package of insurance, often referred to as the business owners' policy. Such a package typically includes:

- **General liability.** This coverage protects the healthcare entity (insured) from liabilities that result from litigation or other losses due to bodily injury or property damage, usually on the healthcare provider's premises.

- **Commercial property.** This policy protects the facilities, including the contents, the building, and related furniture, fixtures, and equipment that support the insured. It considers times of physical loss when a property is damaged or destroyed. Commercial property insurance is the primary source of loss reimbursement.
- **Business income insurance.** This policy helps replace lost income during a crisis period when operating the business is significantly hampered or compromised. While sometimes more difficult to substantiate the claim and convince the insurer that a loss occurred, it is mandatory to have business income insurance within the overall business owners' policy structure.
- **Professional liability.** Liability coverage is essential for healthcare providers. Typically, it entails both an annual aggregate loss plus a per-event loss. Presumably, it covers all applicable professional liability exposure due to an accusation of clinical mistakes, oversights, and unintentional errors. It typically allows for a per-claim maximum coverage along with an annual aggregate amount. It usually carries some allowance for claims made after the insured leaves the practice via employment or partnership status (i.e., the "tail"). It has other requirements of professional conduct and protocols to follow for the insurer to recognize the claim.

Later, we will discuss other insurance types that provide more extensive coverage, particularly in crises. However, as noted above, the business owners' policy components address the primary needs and are essential. These protections are often a single group of policies that allow for economies of scale in the premium pricing. Insurance underwriters will consider the power of volume purchasing and coverage. The exception to this practice is the professional liability policy, which typically stands on its own.

As losses occur, the insurer requires a formal insurance claim notification and often calls for the insurance company to perform its due diligence to determine whether the losses are consistent with the policy terms and conditions. Therefore, the insurer decides whether the claim is legitimate. It is crucial to have a knowledgeable insurance advisor (usually a broker) to represent the insured in procuring its policies and related coverages. As with other pre-planning, the time to assure insurance protections are in place is not when or after a crisis event occurs but before an event occurs. Preplanning and coordination of all insurance coverages should be ongoing as a business management initiative.

Managing a Business Insurance Claim

A business insurance claim is a formal notification to the insurer that advises a loss or damage suffered and the probability of an ensuing claim. Presumably, the request is under the insurance policy, but this is not always guaranteed, as many policies are specific about what they will or will not cover. Specific risks of loss are covered, but often liability claims, such as malpractice and general liability, have clauses in the policy that require certain actions or behaviors that, if not followed, may even negate coverage for specific losses. Therefore, every healthcare provider must have a trusted insurance advisor/broker. That party can ensure the policy covers as much as feasible for the proportionate premium. All insurance companies have a sophisticated underwriting process and agree (or not agree) on certain coverages. More likely, certain coverages will require a higher premium because the risk of loss is more significant to the insurer.

Once a claim is filed, its legitimacy is evaluated. There usually are limits of coverages in property losses and valuation considerations as to the loss of the asset. Liability insurance also has limits of coverage and, in most cases, they are within an aggregate amount per year and an individual claim ceiling. While adjustments to building and asset values occur regularly (primarily for inflation) due to basic cost-of-living and market changes, the insured must know the general effect. They can then use their insurance advisor to guide them through the claims process to maximize the proceeds.

As a result, all healthcare providers, especially providers who own small businesses, should understand the insurance process and ensure the following essential protocols are in place, before and after a crisis event:

- **Plan for adequate coverages and proofs of the insurance claim.** Obtaining a photograph of an accident is not always possible but is beneficial to record and document damages. Consider installing surveillance equipment, including video cameras, to provide possible proof of theft or vandalism.
- **Gather evidence.** If your business experiences a catastrophic event, it is vital to gather as much evidence as possible of damage

and losses. Photographing accidents and disaster events provides the best documentation. Interviewing eyewitnesses and other individuals who were involved is equally essential. Finally, it is critical to inventory your assets—both before and after the incident.

- **Submit losses, as applicable, via police reports.** Anything related to vandalism, a vehicle accident, or theft is included in a police report. This report provides the insurance company with documentation, especially in the event of a crime or a multi-vehicle accident.

- **Communicate with your insurance broker.** Your insurance broker serves as an intermediary/advisor/facilitator of your loss claims. While the decision for coverages lies with the insurer, it still helps to have an advocate who works with that insurer and with you.

- **Review the losses with the adjustor.** Typically, the independent adjustor is looking for a better understanding of the events that apply to the losses. However, he or she may not look deeply for further insights. Therefore, it is essential to communicate with the adjustor as part of the entire claims process.

- **If the losses are large enough, ask a professional to consult and counsel regarding the best way to file and gain reimbursement.** Seek professional assistance from individuals who are "in the business" and know and understand the process when filing major claims. While the insurance broker should be the first source of assistance, going to an outside expert to analyze significant losses is usually beneficial; further, they often pay for themselves with the expanded losses they recover.

- **Consider legal aid.** Using the services of a competent, skilled attorney is advisable when the claims are major and there is doubt about full payment.

- **Get accounting help.** Sometimes it will be necessary to engage a forensic accounting specialist to prove the extent of the losses.

The length of time required to process claims can vary, depending on the number of questions, adjustor's time, and other areas that affect the claim's complexity. Most states mandate by law the length of time an insurance company has to settle and pay a claim. For example, in California, insurers must acknowledge a claim within 15 days of its filing and accept or deny the request within 40 days. If accepted, the insurer must pay out the claim within 30 days of the settlement date.

TYPES OF INSURANCE CLAIMS

Individual losses and claims that involve those losses are often the results of a crisis. Following are specific types of insurance claims.

- **Burglary and theft.** These claims typically involve unauthorized invasion of facilities that result in both loss of specific assets (stolen) and related damages to the facilities. Typically, a deductible must be met before reimbursement of the loss.
- **Water and freeze damage.** While many insurance policies cover losses due to water damage, including natural disasters such as hurricanes, these are specific in their coverage limits and parameters. Likewise, damage to pipes due to freezing may not be covered without specific allowances. Further, they may call for high deductibles.
- **Wind and hail damage.** These "acts of God" are covered by most insurance packages for commercial and residential property. Because they often involve high deductibles, the claim must be significant before the insurer pays anything.
- **Fire.** Damages due to fires can be among the highest claims because a fire often causes significant damage or total destruction of the insured asset. Arson warrants detailed investigations. Fire damage caused by natural events or malfunctions of wiring and the like are usually covered. However, fires are subject to substantial validation by the adjustors.
- **Slips and falls by customers.** These claims are subject to the general liability policy that all businesses must have and keep current. If customers incur injury while on the premises, the insurance company will undoubtedly (through its adjustor) confirm that the "slip and fall" was not due to negligence or some other overt mistake of the insured; even if this is the case, the insurer may pay the claim. Nevertheless, all businesses should ensure that their facilities limit the risk of such events.
- **Customer injury and property damage.** Somewhat akin to slips and falls by customers, the actual injury and property damage while on the business premises should be included within the general liability coverage package.
- **Product liability.** This usually pertains to the manufacturing of products sold to the general public. It requires a specific policy to

address such liability and is subject to the product's production ramifications, overall risks, and more.

- **Reputational harm.** This claim is more nebulous and more challenging to convince an underwriter to provide the coverage for. Many limitations exist and, even then, losses are unclear. Proving reputational harm is a challenge in and of itself.

BUSINESS INTERRUPTION INSURANCE

Business interruption insurance is one of the most crucial insurance coverages because it protects the business when a natural disaster or some other catastrophic event affects business operations. The key to insuring against such losses is having adequate coverage to get the business back in operation. This protection should ensure that the entity can remain viable during a partial or total stoppage period(s).

Companies often underinsure for operational shutdowns because of high premiums and the feeling that the likelihood of a catastrophic loss or interruption in operations is slim. Every company (including all healthcare provider entities) should assess with their insurance broker/consultant whether this insurance is necessary and/or the extent of the coverage. Often, financial reserves that rest with the owners or in the business itself mitigate the need for such insurance. In effect, businesses self-insure up to specific amounts (whether they realize it or not).

The insured should understand what this type of insurance covers, what it does not cover, and at what cost. The insurance should cover the cost of repair and/or replacement of the primary facility, such as the building or equipment that keeps the business going. Usually, owners overlook business interruption insurance until the actual event occurs, wonder what their coverage entails and its limits. A better approach is to be well-informed about what the insurance policy covers and what it excludes. Some form of business interruption coverage is advisable for most entities unless they choose to self-insure.

FORCE MAJEURE AND ITS EFFECTS

The term *force majeure** often refers to "acts of God" that result in significant business losses. Many contractual agreements have force majeure provisions as part of the substance of the contract's terms and conditions. Real estate leases are an excellent example in that this provision attempts to protect the parties from events they cannot control such as damages from war, terrorism, strikes, and quarantines. The contractual provisions apply under such circumstances and protect the party trying to fulfill the contract's terms, including their financial obligations, from unforeseeable events outside of their control.

During the COVID-19 pandemic, various entities used force majeure provisions in their contractual agreements to temporarily decrease and/or abate their financial responsibilities because of their inability to meet contractual deadlines and obligations (including financial). Some force majeure provisions provide complete abatement of financial responsibilities. For example, within a real estate lease for a facility that is no longer functional or in use, such a requirement may allow complete suspension of the lease's obligations. Others provide temporary furlough or reduction in obligations; again, these typically relate to economic terms and conditions.

Force majeure provisions are another form of "insurance" during times of crisis. It is wise to include within every contractual agreement and allow for a specific application that obligates the other party akin to the contractual agreement to suspend or at least significantly reduce the financial obligations during this timeframe. This suspension does not usually negate the debt; rather, it temporarily negates or defers it.

If a party is considering the alternative of invoking a force majeure clause, it must address its potential exposure for damages if (under litigation) as the court determines that the clause does not apply or was invoked improperly. Further, many force majeure clauses in contractual agreements may limit damages, which should be considered before invoking. Some even have certain conditions placed upon the force majeure event, such as requiring performance to resume after a specified period. Recovery of attorneys' fees may also be allowed if the contractual agreement is settled through mediation, arbitration, or an actual lawsuit.

APPROPRIATE INSURANCE AND AMOUNT OF PROTECTION REQUIRED

As we start to summarize our discussion within the context of crisis events and insurance policies, it warrants speaking to whether the business owner (particularly the smaller healthcare provider entity) can be "insurance poor." There is so much cost and so many policies to protect their losses—whether they are in crises or not—that the cost of insurance exceeds the potential risks attempting to cover (or at least mitigate). Again, the insurer should engage a reliable, professional insurance broker/consultant to ensure the "right" amount of insurance coverage without being excessive. Certain losses may be covered through self-insurance where monies are reserved (and safely invested) to cover those potential losses. Such self-insurance does not have to be a formal structure, but merely conceptual in that the business places specific funds for such losses and designates them the traditional "rainy-day fund."

With these above points noted, every healthcare provider (large or small) should ask and answer the questions, "What coverages are needed based upon our vulnerabilities?" and "How much insurance is affordable versus the likelihood of a loss?" Geographical location is a significant factor in answering these questions. For example, if a business is located near a coastal area, the likelihood of damages due to wind and hurricane/tropical storm crises is high. Many lenders that support leases and building purchase/ownership will require insurance for wind and hurricane damage based on the facility's location.

Overall, risk assessment is a fundamental element of evaluating the amount of insurance needed to address a crisis—whether a natural disaster or an event of theft or damages or general or professional liability. It should be systemic to a realistic, reliable, and *affordable* business continuity plan. Healthcare provider businesses that work proactively to review events most likely to occur—whether they are a disaster or otherwise related—those that will trigger an insurance claim will likely be the most adept at dealing with a crisis.

In this chapter, we have considered various threats and their risk of likelihood. Threats include:

- Natural disasters such as tornados, hurricanes, floods, earthquakes, lightning strikes, and wildfires.
- Manmade or technological events like fires and explosions, industrial accidents, chemical/hazardous waste spills, communication and utility outages, system disruptions, and transportation accidents.

- Malicious attacks, including terrorism, bomb threats, vandalism, threats to reputation, protests, civil unrest/riots, robbery, and armed intruders.
- Cyberattacks such as denial of service situations, computer viruses, and the like.
- Workforce downtime or a complete loss, including long-term disabilities, insurance, epidemics (including pandemic events), fatalities, and worker strikes.
- Supply chain disruptions to include counterfeit parts, regulatory requirement violations, and transportation breakdowns.
- Human error due to inadequate training, poor maintenance, carelessness, misconduct, substance abuse, fatigue, and counterfeit parts.

Fundamentally, the entity should undergo a realistic and reasonable evaluation of the risks most significant to the business. Factors include:

- **Historical.** Acknowledgment that history tends to repeat itself.
- **Geographic.** The business's location and proximity to heightened risks of natural disasters such as tornados and hurricanes.
- **Physical.** A certain amount of risk inherent to the services provided.
- **Organizational.** The treatment of diseases and illnesses comes with considerable risk if the assessment and diagnosis are flawed in any way. Thus, professional liability insurance should be the least limited in coverages. This decision requires sound reasoning as to the history of malpractice claims and other related matters, including the malpractice insurance cost. Self-insuring for at least a part of the malpractice coverages could be a suitable alternative.
- **Regulatory.** Risks tied to regulatory constraints and the result of potential losses for non-compliance. It is difficult to get insurance covering all types of losses, mainly due to overt violations or ignorance-based non-compliant conduct.

SUMMARY

Any business can be over-insured. However, with sound reasoning and mitigating the cost of insurance premiums through partial self-funding/reserves along with the use of a trusted insurance consultant advisor, business owners will avoid the common mistake of blindly renewing their insurance policies without taking an assessment of their changing needs. Although over-insuring can put a financial burden on the business, having the insurance in place when a claim event occurs gives relief to the business owner.

During a crisis is *not* the time to evaluate the healthcare provider's insurance coverages. This review should happen regularly (no less than yearly), based upon the parameters we have discussed. Navigating a crisis is stressful and challenging alone. Managing with little or no insurance coverage is exponentially complex. It is wise to complete a thorough assessment of insurance coverages and their ability to mitigate, if not negate, potential losses that result from a crisis.

Force majeure translates literally from French as *superior force*. In English, the term is often used in line with its literal French meaning, but it has other uses, including one with roots in a principle of French law. In business circles, "force majeure" describes those uncontrollable events (such as war, labor stoppages, or extreme weather) that are not the fault of any party and that make it difficult or impossible to carry out regular business. A company may insert a force majeure clause into a contract to absolve itself from liability in the event it cannot fulfill the terms of an agreement (or if attempting to do so will result in loss or damage of goods) for reasons beyond its control.

CHAPTER 13

Post-Crisis Actions

In summarizing crises and crisis management, Bundy et al. state, "Crisis management broadly captures organizational leaders' actions and communication that attempt to reduce the likelihood of a crisis, work to minimize harm from a crisis, and endeavor to reestablish order following a crisis."[1] This final component — investigating how to return to some semblance of normalcy after a crisis — is the focus of this chapter.

Returning to normal operations after a crisis requires an understanding of the current "temperature" of the organization. This discussion will consider internal and external perspectives, effective communication tools, and the interim changes that will need to be made permanent. This chapter provides concerted plans for a wide range of post-crisis actions.

THERMOMETER VERSUS THERMOSTAT

Have you ever been asked if you are a thermometer or a thermostat? This question considers whether a leader **reads** the temperature within their organization (i.e., the thermometer) or **sets** the temperature (i.e., the thermostat). In leadership, the goal is to be a thermostat.

However, post-crisis analyses indicate that leaders often try to be both. They want to read the room when the crisis is at its peak, so they know how to adapt and adjust direction. While successful leaders can do both and still set the tone, ineffective leaders tend to immerse themselves too profoundly in evaluation and miss opportunities to drive the necessary changes. Therefore, as the initial shock of a crisis begins to subside, leaders must return to being a thermostat for their organization.

Consider this example:

The previous leader of a major integrated health system was known for telling the media that his job was to "keep [his] hand on the thermostat" to keep the organization from falling into failure. When this CEO took the reins in 2002, the system was struggling through a merger where the two legacy organizations remained glued to their distinctly different cultures, with no real evidence of integration. The merger intended to improve the health system's financial performance, but that, too, was showing no signs of improvement. **The organization was teetering on the verge of being sold to a for-profit entity.**

As the new CEO evaluated the situation, he sent a memo to all employees as his first action (on his first day in the role). The notice called out the state of affairs: the financial hardship, the upcoming employee layoffs, and the potential sale that may need to be the life raft to keep them afloat. The memo specifically stated that the organization had one "last chance to right the ship." Brutal honesty was uncharacteristic for the organization; the CEO's message opened the eyes of many who did not appreciate the severity of the situation up to that point. Now everyone knew the organization's temperature, and **it helped staff realize the current climate (i.e., the system's performance) would not be sustainable.**

But the CEO did not stop there.

He then called for continual accountability for performance throughout the organization, including published reports to be issued quarterly to show how the organization was running. These reports, which included information on medical errors and clinical operations, were true to his claim of keeping his hand on the thermostat. The reports ensured that all employees knew the organization observed their actions (and the corresponding impact on the organization) and reported them publicly for the world to see. Unsurprisingly, the organization improved by creating a sense of urgency. They frequently and consistently explained where the organization needed to go and capitalized on the unceasing pressure to perform.

The system experienced over $50 million in losses. As the losses lessened, **they were able to break even just two years later**; during that same time, nursing turnover decreased by 13 percentage points. With the pressure on them to perform, the staff took their last chance and often made pains-taking changes to bring the organization back from the brink.

In this situation and others, the logic behind keeping your hand on the thermostat is when the temperature gets too low, there is no sense of urgency to keep people pushing forward, making tough decisions, and continually seeking improvement. The health system in our example found themselves in this situation; **they needed to turn up the temperature to help drive meaningful change**. The inverse is when the temperature gets too high, and people are afraid to take risks, even when they may yield significant benefits to the organization. Thus, a leader must make continual adjustments to ensure the temperature remains right where it needs to be, ensuring the organization is not stagnant or complacent, nor so frenetic it becomes unwieldy.

Finally, just as a leader with a hand on the thermostat is critical, staff who act like thermometers are also crucial. Effective leaders know they need to engage others to function as thermometers, both in times of crisis and not, to provide readings to leadership so they can determine changes to make.

In a crisis, the temperature may have been much too hot for much too long, and yet, perhaps the heat needs to continue to bring closure to the problem. Alternatively, an organization may need a deep freeze to restore order to the organization post-crisis, allowing people to cool down. Once the thermometers indicate where different organization segments are, leaders can use that information to chart a course, communicate it, and make necessary changes. As is standard, reacting appropriately to change, both amid a crisis and during its wind-down, requires a team effort![2]

THE RHYTHM OF A CRISIS: RESOLUTION PHASE

Guidance issued by the CDC[3] identifies a "rhythm" for crises, meaning a predictable flow for how crises emerge, impact, and then recede. The CDC uses four phases to map this rhythm: Preparation, Initial, Maintenance, and Resolution.[3] The associated psychology and required actions are addressed for each of the stages within the rhythm. Figure 13.1 outlines the four main phases and the key considerations for each.[4]

Initial, and Maintenance); here, we address the final phase: Resolution. Framing the post-crisis actions as "resolution" may convey a sense of finality to some; however, crisis management is better thought of as a circle in which the Resolution phase gives immediate way to the Preparation phase. Only through this continuous diligence and improvement can organizations ensure their most effective

FIGURE 13.1. The Crisis and Emergency Risk Communication (CERC) Rhythm[4]

Preparation	Initial	Maintenance	Resolution
•Draft and test messages •Develop partnerships •Create plans •Determine approval process	•Express empathy •Explain risks •Promote action •Describe response efforts	•Explain ongoing risks •Segment audiences •Provide background information •Address rumors	•Motivate vigilance •Discuss lessons learned •Revise plan

preparedness and response when needed. The applications of the Resolution phase are listed in Figure 13.2.

The National Research Council's work on how we learn from disasters centers focuses on three significant activities: acquiring post-disaster data, sharing post-disaster data, and capitalizing on enhanced awareness.[5] This assessment is a helpful complement to the CERC resources and highlights the need for data collection and sharing as an integral part of the post-crisis workflow. Depending on the type of crisis, the data collected may be more quantitative or qualitative and may include the perspectives of internal stakeholders, external stakeholders, or both. This aspect of the post-crisis processing should not be overlooked.

ORGANIZATIONAL LEARNING AND SOCIAL EVALUATIONS

The internal and external perspectives within each of the three main stages of a crisis—pre-crisis prevention, crisis management, and post-crisis outcomes—should receive careful consideration (see Figure 13.3).[1]

Within the post-crisis outcomes stage, the NRC's research focuses on organizational learning as a critical component of processing inter-

FIGURE 13.2. Applications of CERC Resolution Phase

Key Consideration	Application
Motivate people to take action or remain vigilant.	Given the impact on your medical practice, staff, patients, and/or community stakeholders, it is appropriate to first express empathy for those who may have suffered trauma, loss of security, or loss of physical property. Take time to reach out to those who have been affected and express your support for them. Next, meet with appropriate parties and message, in clear terms, what needs to be done next. If it is time to "turn up the heat" or "cool things down," this needs to be communicated to stakeholders so they know what is expected of them.
Promote community preparedness for possible future crises.	Coming off a significant crisis provides a burning platform for discussions about the future. Use this opportunity to explain to stakeholders why change must happen *now*, to ensure issues will be less stressful or more prepared for next time. Enlist their help in the actions that need to be taken.
Discuss, document, and share lessons learned from the response.	Organize debriefing sessions to solicit and record myriad stakeholders' reactions to and lessons learned from the crisis. Every applicable department should be considered, from the front desk team to providers, to avoid missing valuable insights. These sessions should be constructive and devoid of emotion or finger-pointing to the greatest extent possible. However, the dialog must be robust to fully capture where there may be exposures, errors, or problems to be remedied.
Evaluate plans.	Evaluate the crisis plan (if one existed before the crisis). If such a document does not exist, take the time to develop it now. Then, review it in the context of the immediate past crisis. By walking through the plan in a tabletop exercise and using a real-life example, evaluate the plan and revise where necessary.

nal perspectives and social evaluations as a vital component of processing external perspectives.

INTERNAL PERSPECTIVE: ORGANIZATIONAL LEARNING

Before the COVID-19 pandemic, 20% of physicians engaged in telehealth. A mere eight weeks after the pandemic became prevalent in

FIGURE 13.3. Internal and External Perspectives of the Crisis Process[1]

	Pre-Crisis Prevention	Crisis Management	Post-Crisis Outcomes
Internal Perspective	Organizational Preparedness	Crisis Leadership	Organizational Learning
External Perspective	Stakeholder Relationships	Stakeholder Perceptions	Social Evaluations

the United States, survey data indicated that 63% of physicians had adopted telehealth. This sharp increase in the use of an existing, but not pervasive, technology was one of many changes organizations made as they adapted to the crises of the pandemic. Additional research indicated that 60% of physicians who are currently using telehealth intend to continue using it in the future.

For many people, the disruption in clinical care delivery was one of the more significant *positive* outcomes of the pandemic. A massive retooling to providing healthcare services using telemedicine increased access for specific segments of the population by video and text and the widespread adoption of a relatively new modality that providers can use to reach and assist their patients.

Identifying telehealth as an effective response to the changing delivery of healthcare services during the COVID-19 pandemic was an "aha" moment. It highlights a critical action item for leaders to consider as they prepare for their next crisis: What changes did we make during this crisis that were important to our near-term future success? Merely identifying the changes made helps open the door to crucial learnings for leaders to discover and prepare for what happens next.

Evaluating Changes Made

Developing an in-depth understanding of the changes made during (and as an immediate result of) a crisis should be one of the initial post-stabilization activities healthcare delivery systems complete. This identification is essential in helping the organization prepare for and ultimately deal with the next crisis. However, detecting the changes is only the first step to preparing; leaders must then take that information and evaluate the changes to see if they are worth implementing permanently or if there is a lesson to learn about why this change influenced the crisis' outcomes.

Leadership can ask a series of questions in that evaluation process to help guide the assessment and uncover truths:

1. What changes made during a crisis have improved the organization (employees, operating efficiency, clinical services, financial performance, etc.) during and after the crisis?
2. How do we know those specific changes resulted in an improvement?
3. What data or other results quantify the relative improvements those changes made?
4. Why were those changes so beneficial?
5. What made those changes necessary?
6. Which of those changes are we interested in making a permanent fixture in the organization?
7. Why are we interested in making those changes permanent?
8. What are the necessary resources to make those changes permanent?
9. What is the anticipated impact of making those changes permanent?
10. What evaluation process will we use to monitor the impact of those changes in the future to ensure they are as relevant post-crisis as they were mid-crisis?

As we continue our telehealth example, it is crucial to understand the reasons for the massive uptick in use during the pandemic and what benefits it created. Arguably, this is more important than the simple recognition that it happened, as it speaks to what needs to occur next.[2]

However, in reality, there also can be a reluctance to learning from the emergency. For example, Haunschild et al.[6] contend that organizations tend to learn and they tend to forget. In their studies of events triggered by serious errors (including NASA's Challenger and Columbia accidents, as well as serious pharmaceutical errors such as Merck's withdrawal of Vioxx from the market in 2004), they concluded that organizations focus on their current, most pressing priorities and, therefore, lessons from prior experiences may be forgotten. This work highlights the need to evaluate the changes that were made in response to a crisis and reinforcement of the new processes that may be implemented as a result.

EXTERNAL PERSPECTIVE: SOCIAL EVALUATIONS

Responding to Changes Made

Although it may seem evident that telehealth will be one of the more lasting changes to come out of this pandemic, it is not without challenges. Some people call this period "The Great Acceleration," given the massive shifts it has furthered in telehealth, e-commerce, cloud computing, and reshoring, among others.

For example, despite the ambition of the current telehealth users and their reported commitment to the platform in advancing care, 35% of Americans do not have broadband internet access. This makes real-time telehealth via videoconferencing or another data-heavy program difficult, if not impossible.[7]

For all the progress since mid-March 2020, those changes are not perfect. Research indicates that asynchronous communication (like texting) may be the most impactful approach to leveling the field for more people to benefit from telehealth. To be clear, it is doubtful that asynchronous communication is the only solution, but rather, it indicates that it should be part of the more global future solution. Meaning, organizations should applaud themselves for synchronous communication and care, but the progress should not stop there.

Using our telehealth example, after identifying and realizing the impact of telehealth (it brought care to patients where they lived), the challenge is figuring out how to continue to care for patients wherever they are, including in locations where broadband is not available. For many organizations, this may mean maintaining a robust telemedicine program that includes both real-time and asynchronous care. Providing these options may help ensure patient access to healthcare, regardless of their access to reliable internet.

The process of robust assessment, considering external perspectives, and continual search for solutions builds on initial successes during a crisis and helps organizations prepare for their next situation, whatever form it takes.

ISSUES TO CONSIDER IF YOUR PRACTICE IS SEVERELY DAMAGED OR DESTROYED

The four primary characteristics of crises are:
1. Sources of *uncertainty, disruption, and change.*
2. *Harmful or threatening* for organizations and their stakeholders, many of whom may have conflicting needs and demands.
3. *Behavioral phenomena,* meaning that the literature has recognized that crises are socially constructed by the actors involved rather than a function of the depersonalized factors of an objective environment.
4. Parts of larger *processes* rather than discrete events.[1]

In some cases, the "harmful" aspects of crises result in the damage or destruction of physical property.

Damage Assessment

Figure 13.4, adapted from the University of Memphis crisis management plan,[8] provides a prescriptive plan for completing a comprehensive damage assessment. This step is necessary as the crisis closes. Interestingly, this builds upon the EOC structure discussed in Chapter 6 and highlights the need for a comprehensive, documented plan for crisis response. Before an organization can move forward, it must first assess what damage has occurred and its extent. With this information, they can then move forward with remediation.

SITE INVENTORY – GOODS, MATERIALS, AND EQUIPMENT

Using the University of Memphis' crisis management plan[8] as the basis, Figure 13.5 identifies an actionable plan for completing a site inventory. As with the damage assessment, this is another critical component of post-crisis activity. However, the site inventory taken post-crisis is most helpful when compared against a site inventory, taken pre-crisis, to identify differences. This inventory provides another solid example

FIGURE 13.4. Actionable Process for Assessing Damage

Primary Responsibilities
- Manage the collection, evaluation, and calculation of damage information and loss estimates.
- Provide current and ongoing damage estimates to the Emergency Operations Center (EOC).
- Provide estimates of content loss for buildings and facilities.
- Identify salvage opportunities for content and assets.
- Prepare reports for the Preliminary Damage Assessment (PDA) report for submission to FEMA.
- Support inspections and emergency repair with estimates for emergency projects.
- Support FEMA/Recovery Team Leader with damage estimates and summaries to support application and program eligibility.
- Manage the inspections, posting, reporting, and documentation of buildings and facilities.
- Coordinate with Physical Plant Unit Response Center to deploy the Building Inspection Teams.

Actions
1. When aware of or notified the organization is responding to a large emergency or crisis, contact police services and/or EOC to confirm activation of the Planning Section.
2. If activated, report to the EOC. Sign in with the EOC Administration staff. Immediately get a report on emergency conditions and situations. Begin a log of your activities and keep it current throughout the emergency response.
3. Verify with the Planning Section Chief the type of assessment needed:
    a. Loss estimates are generally based on damage to known value which results in a loss.
    b. Repair/reconstruction estimates are based on projects and restoration estimates and are higher than losses.
    c. Financial impacts include loss of revenue, inventory, medical, fees, liability and/or other incurred expenses.
    d. Initial damage assessment reports are usually a calculation of loss. However, FEMA program information may include the other costs, as appropriate.
4. DO NOT RELEASE DAMAGE ASSESSMENT INFORMATION OUTSIDE OF THE EOC UNLESS APPROVED BY THE EOC MANAGEMENT TEAM.
5. As damage becomes known and inspection reports are available, prepare summary reports on the status of buildings, facilities, and systems and the estimated dollar amounts of damage. The following criteria may be used in the general assessment of damage to buildings and facilities:
    a. Building Value (may be known).
    b. Estimated damage percent.
    c. Calculation of loss based on value or replacement value per square foot.
    d. Calculation of loss of contents based on value or replacement value.
    e. Calculation of cost of repair to utilities.

(figure continues)

FIGURE 13.4. Actionable Process for Assessing Damage *(continued)*

6. If there will be a delay before the inspections, teams are ready to be deployed, coordinate with the Operations Section to send out teams to conduct rapid surveys of the campus to ascertain the general condition of buildings, roads, and utilities. If the URCs are not activated, have the teams communicate directly with you or the Operations Section via cell phones or radios. These teams do not need special training, they are to report only on what they see and not enter buildings or hazardous areas.

7. Determine how many Building Inspection Teams will be needed. If the URCs do not have sufficient staff, work with the URCs and the Logistics Section Chief to activate contracted services of engineers. The contractors should report to the URCs for assignments.

8. Check with Physical Plant to determine if a building manager or other physical plant staff will be available in the field to meet the Inspection Teams.

9. Keep track of building inspections and forward to Situation Status. Maintain a list or keep track on the map. Note the color of placards and tags of buildings. For hazardous buildings (red tagged), forward to the Operations Section for security operations.

10. If the disaster is an earthquake, be prepared to send Building Inspection Teams to re-inspect buildings following any aftershocks.

11. Identify the departments and occupants of damaged buildings. As able, estimate damage and loss to contents and assets – AS AN ESTIMATE FOR PRELIMINARY REPORTS. If able, contact department representatives to get general reports of contents and/or damage. Please note that detailed information on actual losses must be obtained from each school or department and will be needed to complete either FEMA Disaster Assistance Program applications or insurance reimbursement. Forward all detailed information to the department that will manage the recovery and replacement of lost and damaged assets.

12. Keep track of damage assessment and loss estimation on a spreadsheet and list by building or address. Update as information becomes available.

13. Provide damage summary reports by FEMA categories, if requested. The categories are (based on current application forms – this may change in the future):
    a. Category A: Debris removal
    b. Category B: Emergency protective measures
    c. Category C: Road systems and bridges
    d. Category D: Water control facilities
    e. Category E: Public buildings and contents
    f. Category F: Public utilities
    g. Category G: Parks, recreational, and other

Deactivation and Recovery
- Forward all documentation to the Finance/Administration Section Chief for post-disaster recovery documentation.
- Provide necessary documentation to Insurance/Claims EOC representative for claims on insured properties.

FIGURE 13.5. Actionable Process for Site Inventory

Primary Responsibilities

- Inventory the organization's major supplies and equipment.
- Allocate the organization's supplies and equipment, as needed.
- Provide for all logistical arrangements for delivery and use of organization's supplies and equipment.
- Request the purchasing of additional supplies and equipment to support emergency operations and augment depleted supplies.

Actions

1. When aware of or notified, the organization is responding to a large emergency or crisis, contact Police Services and/or EOC to confirm activation of the Logistics Section.
2. If activated, report to the EOC. Sign in. Immediately get a report on emergency conditions and situations. Begin a log of your activities and keep it current throughout the emergency response.
3. With the Logistics Section members, assess the damage, impacts, and response operations to identify the potential need for resources—both immediate and in the recovery period. Identify the use of and need for supplies and equipment. Develop a list of needed items and estimate location and time needed.
4. Conduct a general inventory of all available material resources at the organization. This includes fuel, food, equipment, and supplies. Work with departments and Unit Response Centers to access resources and support services for the emergency response and recovery operations.
5. Develop an action plan for the provision of materials, goods, and equipment in support of emergency operations. Provide for all logistics including transportation, delivery, receipt, and dissemination of materials, goods, and equipment. If the organization does not have sufficient inventory to support operations, work with the Logistics Section Chief and the Resources Procurement staff to procure resources.
6. Track the delivery and utilization of supplies. If the emergency response phase will be prolonged, plan for the purchase of additional supplies to continue emergency support and replace used inventory.
7. Ensure the organization's operators of equipment are trained in the safe use and operation of the equipment. It may be necessary to contract certified operators if the organization does not have staff available.
8. As emergency operations subside, track the return of equipment and unused supplies to the departments and owners. Coordinate the return of all rentals and leased equipment.

Deactivation and Recovery

9. Forward all documentation of materials, goods, and equipment used in the emergency response to the Finance/Administration Section.

of where preparation is a critical component of the overall crisis management process.

POST-DISASTER CHECKLISTS

The Department of Health & Human Services Assistant Secretary for Preparedness and Response (ASPR) developed the Technical Resources, Assistance Center, and Information Exchange (TRACIE) to help connect and inform members of the healthcare industry. TRACIE has published a compendium of available resources for post-disaster response as part of their available resources. The summary includes three key sections: checklists for healthcare facilities to use before repopulating their facility, post-disaster assessment tools for healthcare facilities, and other resources to guide the post-disaster activities.[8] The comprehensive listing of resources identified by ASPR TRACIE, is available for use across hospitals and medical practices as part of their crisis plans, are noted below.

1. Hospital/Healthcare Repopulation

- California Hospital Association. (2020). Hospital Repopulation After Evacuation: Guidelines and Checklist. (Accessed 5/27/2021.):

  www.calhospitalprepare.org/post/hospital-repopulation-after-evacuation-guidelines-and-checklist

  The California Hospital Association worked with subject matter experts to identify best practices and regulatory agency requirements that must be considered when repopulating after the total or partial evacuation of general acute care hospital inpatient buildings. The guide includes a checklist that can be completed electronically or printed and filled out by hand.

- Centers for Disease Control and Prevention. (2013). Remediation and Infection Control Considerations for Reopening Healthcare Facilities Closed Due to Extensive Water and Wind Damage. (Accessed 5/27/2021.):

  www.cdc.gov/disasters/reopen_healthfacilities.html

  This webpage provides information to help healthcare facilities with the tasks involved with cleaning up and reopening healthcare facilities after a natural disaster. It includes checklists for mold remediation and structural recovery, water and electrical utilities, ventilation system, structural building materials, medical equipment, certification for occupancy, and post-reoccupation surveillance.

2. Hospital/Healthcare Post-Disaster Assessment Resources

- American College of Emergency Physicians. Hospital Disaster Preparedness Self-Assessment Tool. (Accessed 5/27/2021.):

  www.calhospitalprepare.org/sites/main/files/file-attachments/hospital_disaster_preparedness_self-assessment_tool.doc

  This detailed checklist assessment can help hospital staff review their emergency management programs. This tool includes information on categories that should be considered in a post-disaster assessment (particularly sections 3-7).

- California Emergency Medical Services Authority. (2014). Hospital Incident Command System 251- Facility Systems Status Report. (Accessed 5/27/2021.):

  https://emsa.ca.gov/wp-content/uploads/sites/71/2017/07/HICS-251-Facility-System-Status-Report_4.docx

  This HICS form is to be used to determine the status (functional, partially functional, nonfunctional) of a healthcare facility after an emergency event.

- Centers for Disease Control and Prevention. Checklist for Infection Control Concerns When Reopening Healthcare Facilities Closed Due to Extensive Water and Wind Damage. (Accessed 5/27/2021.)

  www.cdc.gov/disasters/reopen_healthfacilities_checklist.html

  This checklist guides in completing building and life safety inspections prior to restoration work and guidance for infection control review of facilities to be done before the hospital can reopen. Attachment A includes a site-specific checklist for selected areas of the facility (e.g., laboratory, pharmacy).

- Florida Health Care Association. Post-Storm Recovery Planning Considerations. (Accessed 5/27/2021.)

www.ltcprepare.org/sites/default/files/Rev%20Recovery%20Plan ning%20Considerations.pdf

This document provides post-storm recovery guidance and checklists for nursing homes and long-term care facilities.

- Pan American Health Organization, World Health Organization. (2017). Hospital Administrator, Post Disaster Functional Checklist. (Accessed 8/24/2021.)

  https://iris.paho.org/bitstream/handle/10665.2/34978/Hospital Checklist_eng.pdf?sequence=1&isAllowed=y

  This checklist is for use by a CEO or Hospital Administrator within 24 hours after the impact of a natural or man-made disaster. Its objective is to determine the immediate level of safety and functionality of the hospital. The facility assessment is in three segments: structural, non-structural, and functional capacity.

- Raske, K. (2006). Greater New York Hospital Association. Greater New York Hospital Association Recovery Checklist for Hospitals After a Disaster. (Accessed 5/27/2021.)

  www.gnyha.org/tool/recovery-checklist-for-hospitals-after-a-disaster/

  Hospital staff can utilize this facility recovery checklist to check for potential issues in the facility after a disaster.

- Zane R, Biddinger P, Gerteis J, Hassol A. (2010). Hospital Assessment and Recovery Guide. AHRQ Publication No. 10-0081. (Accessed 5/27/2021.)

  https://archive.ahrq.gov/prep/hosprecovery/hosprecovery.pdf

  This guide helps organize the initial assessment of a hospital after an evacuation/closure due to an emergency event. Each of its 11 sections has its own team and assessment assignment: Administration, Facilities, Security and Fire Safety, Information Technology and Communications, Biomedical Engineering, Medical, Ancillary Services, Materials Management, Building and Grounds Maintenance/ Environmental Services, and Support Services.

3. Other Resources

- Hassol, A., Zane, R. (2006). Reopening Shuttered Hospitals to Expand Surge Capacity. AHRQ Publication No. 06-0029. (Accessed 5/27/201.)

  https://archive.ahrq.gov/research/shuttered/

  This guidance document provides tools and recommendations to help planners determine if and how to utilize an abandoned or shuttered hospital for surge capacity needs during a mass casualty or another similar event. It provides staffing requirements, safety checklists, supplies and equipment needs, and regulatory/legal issues to consider.

- Harvard School of Public Health, Emergency Preparedness and Response Exercise Program. Essential Functions and Considerations for Hospital Recovery Version 2. Federal Emergency Management Agency. (Accessed 5/27/2021.)

  http://docplayer.net/15275997-Essential-functions-and-considerations-for-hospital-recovery.html

  This document helps hospitals prepare to manage recovery from all types of events. Recovery planning benchmarks start on page 34 to help hospitals independently assess their recovery capabilities. The benchmarks are drawn from various sources, including the ASPR Healthcare Preparedness and Response Capabilities, Joint Commission Hospital Accreditation Standards, the National Disaster Response Force (NDRF), and lessons learned from both recovery-focused exercises and real-world disasters. The document also includes questions to consider during recovery planning starting on page 38.

- South Carolina Department of Health and Environmental Control. (2016). Post-Disaster Hospital Reopening Procedures. Accessed:

  http://www.scdhec.gov/Health/Docs/POST-DISASTER_HOSPITAL_REOPENING_PROCEDURES.pdf

  This document provides a step-by-step guide for hospitals to follow prior to reopening. It includes five primary steps with action items under each.

While some of these resources are national, others have state-specific contact information. Check with your state and local agencies to ensure appropriate contact information for local bodies. Ensure this information is documented within the disaster plan and will be immediately accessible when needed.

SUMMARY

Crises test every one of us as leaders, and it is only when we have made it through that we can appreciate how very real of a challenge it is to lead in times of crisis. As discussed above, there are a series of actions to be taken amid crisis and, once it passes to ensure we lead as effectively as possible. However, it is equally, if not more, important to consider the preparatory actions to take before the next crisis arises. Leading in times of crisis can be a challenge and without significant preparation, it will be even more challenging. By appropriately completing the post-crises assessments, it will enable better preparation for the future.

RESOURCES

1. Bundy J, Pfarrer MD, Short CE, Coombs WT. Crises and Crisis Management: Integration, Interpretation, and Research Development. *Journal of Management.* 2017;43(6):1661-1692. doi:10.1177/0149206316680030
2. Greeter A. Leading in Crisis: How to Prepare, How to Execute, How to Thrive. Coker Group. October 2020. https://cokergroup.com/wp-content/uploads/2020/10/Leading-in-Crisis_How-to-Prepare-Execute-and-Thrive.pdf. Accessed May 27, 2021.
3. Centers for Disease Control and Prevention. Introduction. Crisis + Emergency Risk Communication. 2019. p. 5. Accessed May 27, 2021. https://emergency.cdc.gov/cerc/ppt/CERC_CommunityEngagement.pdf. Accessed June 9, 2021.
4. Centers for Disease Control and Prevention. Psychology of a Crisis. Crisis + Emergency Risk Communication. 2019; p. 13. https://emergency.cdc.gov/cerc/ppt/CERC_Psychology_of_a_Crisis.pdf. Accessed May 27, 2021.
5. National Research Council. A Safer Future: Reducing the Impacts of Natural Disasters. Washington, DC: The National Academies Press; 1991. https://doi.org/10.17226/1840. Accessed May 27, 2021.
6. Haunschild P, Polidoro F, & Chandler D. Organizational Oscillation Between Learning and Forgetting: The Dual Role of Serious Errors. *Organization Science.* 26(6): 1682-1701. http://www.jstor.org/stable/43663677. Accessed April 12, 2021.
7. Nusca A. FCC: 35% of Americans Don't Have Broadband Internet Access. ZDNet. February 24, 2010. https://www.zdnet.com/article/fcc-35-of-americans-dont-have-broadband-internet-access. Accessed June 29, 2021.

8. The University of Memphis. Crisis Management Plan: April 2020. www.memphis.edu/crisis/pdf/crisis_mgmt_plan.pdf. Accessed May 27, 2021.
9. ASPR TRACIETechnical Assistance Request. https://asprtracie.s3.amazonaws.com/documents/aspr-tracie-ta---healthcare-facilities-engineering-evac-checklists---7-31-18.pdf. Accessed May 27, 2021.

CHAPTER 14

Averting Repeated Challenges

If I had it to do over, what would I do differently?

Although disasters are devastating, many of our advances and innovative lessons result from a crisis. For example, when Hurricane Katrina struck New Orleans in August 2005, most hospitals and medical practices lost all their medical records. The floodwaters damaged the computers, losing all patient data. Vital information, such as medical histories, allergies, and drug-to-drug interactions, were unknown, making it difficult and dangerous to treat patients.

Surprisingly, many national pharmacies in New Orleans (Walgreens, Rite-Aid, and others) continued to operate with little disruption. Countless hospitals had to request data from major pharmacies to recreate their destroyed medical records.

So, what was different in the preparedness? The major pharmacies operating in New Orleans were using an offsite data center from their corporate offices outside of Louisiana. After Katrina, cloud computing began to take off. Coastal cities were among the first enterprises to adopt cloud computing—for obvious reasons. Only a few coastal practices still run servers in their local office.

LEARNING FROM OUR MISTAKES

No one wants to experience a crisis, yet if you must go through a disaster, it is critical to learn from it. One of the most underrated functions of a crisis is having the chance to look back at mistakes and/or unforeseen outcomes. Here are some common lessons:

1. **Simple things matter.** For example, a minor fire (even one under control) in a breakroom can turn into a major disas-

ter if it sets off the building's sprinkler system. This disaster can become significantly worse if a sprinkler head is in the computer room. Most experts disable sprinkler heads in their computer rooms and replace them with an oxygen suppressor to avoid water damage to expensive equipment. It is also crucial to confirm that the sprinkler system is in zones, so the devices only activate in the area where there is a fire. Older sprinkler systems could flood an entire building in response to a burning bag of popcorn.

2. **Do not wait for a disaster to discover that all your important documents are still in the office.** Store essential documents offsite in a fireproof filing cabinet. Make a second and third set of these documents and keep them in different places for added security. Scan and upload documents and back them up to an offsite server as a backup to the backup. Access to critical documents will be essential during and after the crisis.

3. **Review your insurance coverage frequently.** Policies can change, and so can their terms. Never wait until after a disaster to decide what to cover. For example, most cybersecurity policies do NOT cover a loss if the practice violated a HIPAA rule. (See Chapter 12 for more information about insurance considerations.)

4. **There is no excuse for not having a plan.** The worse outcomes happen when there is no plan. Not having a plan creates chaos and confusion and leads to costly mistakes.

5. **Practice, practice, practice.** A crisis does not come with advance notice, so be prepared. Run fire drills, hold mock active shooter drills, practice evacuating the building, and conduct other exercises. Again, your insurance policy may require you to demonstrate that you have a functioning readiness posture when they consider claims.

6. **Have cash on hand.** Depending on the type of disaster, banks and ATMs could be disabled. Even credit card machines can go down. We recommend one of the physician-owners keep up to $10,000 in a locked safe at their home to cover emergency expenses.

7. **Have a hard copy list of the following information:**
   - Staff phone numbers and next of kin

- Key emergency contact information
- Vendor and suppliers contact information

One lesson from EVERY disaster is the difficulty with communication. Searching for information in a crisis can be stressful.

8. **Document critical infrastructure about your office space.** Know where and how to shut off power and water. Know the storm drains' location(s) and have the tools necessary to unclog them if this is a known issue. Have your fire escape plan documented and posted. Identify a safe place to meet so you can easily account for staff. Ensure that all doors and windows operate correctly and can be opened easily in the event of an emergency.

9. **Have proper tools on hand.** For example, some water shutoff valves require a specific tool to turn off. Now would be an excellent time to verify if you have this tool. (See checklist below for a complete list of tools.)

10. **The key to being prepared is education and awareness during regular times.**

Avoid previous errors in planning, preparation, and implementation. This principle goes hand and hand with learning from mistakes, but one additional action is to redesign any flaws in the previous plan that lead to an unfavorable outcome. Catastrophes never show up with a pre-defined playbook. Some events take a life of their own and can evolve for the better or worse in real-time. Therefore, build a plan capable of adapting to changing circumstances. For example, the response to a hurricane warning will differ significantly from a mandatory evacuation. When the evacuation notice sounds, someone must oversee removing the vaccines from the refrigerator and placing them into an ice chest, so they do not ruin when the power goes out. This pivot is an example of a significant shift from readiness to evacuation.

IMPORTANT ITEMS TO HAVE ON HAND

The following are important Items to have on hand. The Department of Homeland Security offers guidance for what is considers a "basic" disaster supply kit. The online version is available at www.Ready.gov. Although the list is updated frequently, these are the recommendations as of 2020.

BASIC DISASTER SUPPLIES KIT

Store items in your supply kit in airtight plastic bags and put your entire disaster supplies kit in one or two easy-to-carry containers, such as plastic bins or a duffel bag. A basic emergency supply kit could include the following:

- Water (https://www.ready.gov/water; one gallon per person per day for at least three days, for drinking and sanitation)
- Food (https://www.ready.gov/food; at least a three-day supply of non-perishable food)
- Battery-powered or hand-crank radio and a NOAA Weather Radio with tone alert
- Flashlight
- First aid kit
- Extra batteries
- Whistle (to signal for help)
- Dust mask (to help filter contaminated air)
- Plastic sheeting and duct tape (to shelter in place; https://www. ready.gov/shelter)
- Moist towelettes, garbage bags, and plastic ties (for personal sanitation)
- Wrench or pliers (to turn off utilities; https://www.ready.gov/ safety-skills)
- Manual can opener (for food)
- Local maps
- Cell phone with chargers and a backup battery
- Download the Recommended Supplies List (PDF; https://www. ready.gov/sites/default/files/2020-03/ready_emergency-supply-kit-checklist.pdf)

ADDITIONAL EMERGENCY SUPPLIES

Since the Spring of 2020, the CDC has recommended keeping additional items in their emergency kits to prevent the spread of coronavirus or other viruses and influenza.

Consider adding the following items to your emergency supply kit based on your individual needs:

- Cloth face coverings (*for everyone ages two and above*), soap, hand sanitizer, disinfecting wipes to disinfect surfaces (https://www.cdc.gov/coronavirus/2019-ncov/prevent-getting-sick/diy-cloth-face-coverings.html)
- Prescription medications (https://www.ready.gov/individuals-access-functional-needs)
- Non-prescription medications, such as pain relievers, antidiarrheals, antacids, or laxatives
- Prescription eyeglasses and contact lens solution
- Infant formula, bottles, diapers, wipes, and diaper rash cream
- Pet food and extra water for your pets
- Cash or traveler's checks
- Important family documents, such as copies of insurance policies, identification, and bank account records, saved electronically or in a waterproof, portable container
- Sleeping bag or a warm blanket for each person
- Complete change of clothing appropriate for your climate and sturdy shoes
- Fire extinguisher
- Matches in a waterproof container
- Feminine supplies and personal hygiene items
- Mess kits, paper cups, plates, paper towels, and plastic utensils
- Paper and pencil
- Books, games, puzzles, or other activities for children

MAINTAINING YOUR EMERGENCY KIT

After assembling your kit, remember to maintain it, so it is ready when needed:

- Keep canned food in a cool, dry place.
- Store boxed food in a tightly closed plastic or metal containers.
- Replace expired items, as required.
- Re-think your needs every year and update your kit as your family's needs change.

KIT STORAGE LOCATIONS

Since you do not know where you will be when an emergency occurs, prepare supplies for home, work, and cars.

- **Home:** Keep this kit in a designated place and have it ready if you must leave your house quickly. Make sure all family members know the location of the paraphernalia.
- **Work:** Be prepared to shelter at work for at least 24 hours. Your work kit should include food, water, and other necessities like medicines, as well as comfortable walking shoes, stored in a "grab-and-go" case.
- **Car.** In case you are stranded, keep a kit of emergency supplies in your vehicle (https://www.ready.gov/car).

Source: www.ready.gov/kit

SUMMARY

We realize from a crisis such as the events of 2020 that whatever the category of the event, we make mistakes in execution. "If we had it to again, we would. . . ." is the question to ask. What would we do differently to prepare for the unexpected? There are mistakes to avert and improvements to make. Here are a few principles we have addressed to prevent future oversights.

1. Prepare for the worst.
2. Keep things simple and develop everyone's skillsets.
3. Check over your insurance coverage—frequently.
4. Maintain cash offsite.
5. Make copies of contact lists and crucial documents and maintain them in several places to protect vital data.
6. Prepare emergency plans and conduct drills for various scenarios.
7. Know what supplies and tools to have on hand for office, home, and vehicle.
8. Maintain and store your emergency kits.

These are just a few of the preparations necessary to avoid repeated mistakes in the event of crises. Be ready! Expect the unexpected to occur and for it to be worse than you thought!

CHAPTER 15

Summary

PREPARATION AND PLANNING

Regardless how one defines a crisis, every individual and organization will inevitably experience challenges that entail some form of crisis at some point. Planning and preparation are not just important—they are essential. No one wants to be scrounging for ammunition in the middle of a gunfight. You must be ready to face a crisis before it arrives. Likewise, crisis preparation should not be something that occurs amid the chaos and uncertainty that inevitably accompanies a severe situation. As such, organizations must have general plans in place to survive a chaotic environment. These plans do not have to be specific to a particular crisis; instead, they should define protocols and procedures for dealing with a broad range of emergencies or critical problems. Before a catastrophe occurs, have a backup plan in place.

According to the ancient proverb "Desperate times call for desperate measures," actions that might seem extreme under normal circumstances are appropriate during adversity. Most crises are unplanned, but some form of problem for every organization, including all healthcare-related entities, is inevitable. So, the prospect and general premise of preparation for crises should be applied via a predictable, preventable, and well-planned vulnerability assessment. Conducting a complete vulnerability assessment before developing a crisis preparedness plan will allow the healthcare organization to identify probable and predictable crises. In some cases, completing this preparedness process may minimize the severity of a crisis.

Following some of these key steps can result in significant value when thinking about planning and preparation for a crisis:
1. Designate a crisis team.
2. Create a vulnerability assessment tool.
3. Analyze results and develop scenarios.
4. Develop a comprehensive crisis communications plan.

DAY-TO-DAY CRISIS MANAGEMENT

Chapter 3 considered approaches for navigating crises through the ongoing management of day-to-day medical practice operations. Faced with an unprecedented health crisis and a growing economic calamity that we have encountered throughout the COVID-19 pandemic, leaders have been challenged to manage the day-to-day operations while trying to navigate unprecedented conditions. In confronting these trials, leaders quickly learned how critical it is to be proactive and not reactive. Further, we have realized that it is also necessary to lead—not just manage. Some of the fundamental leadership principles during a crisis include staying true to your organization's purpose, continually striving to build trust, and investing in others.

Noting the meaningful and straightforward point by Benjamin Franklin, "If you fail to plan, you are planning to fail," we must consider some key planning steps continued from the first chapter:

1. Develop backup documentation procedures.
2. Have an evacuation plan.
3. Test your plans and refine them based on the test results.
4. Be prepared with infrastructure and procedures for working remotely.
5. Have a thoroughly tested contingency plan in place and ready for deployment across the entire organization.

Other considerations for day-to-day management and leadership during a crisis include the need for a designated team leading the crisis response and implementing a clear chain of command. Also, there should be a defined communications protocol in place to implement both within the organization and externally to the public, customers, et al. Finally, we must consider how the management of critical workflows will be managed and establish a designated process for managing people.

COMMUNICATIONS DURING AND AFTER A CRISIS

One of the most critical and often poorly addressed components of any crisis is communications. If we are honest, we likely will find that one of the most significant pitfalls for organizations, in general, can be poor communications. However, the importance of effective communications could easily and quickly worsen the already high levels of severity entailed with many crises. Exceptional leaders are always effective communicators, creating an environment that fosters stability and support.

When it comes to communications, it is crucial to provide a clear message, ensuring no uncertainty or miscommunication in the information. Even outside the context of a crisis, people look to an organization's leaders for clear, concise insight into what is happening. It is critical, therefore, to impart a sense of confidence in the message you are relaying.

As previously stated, communications can pose challenges for leaders within an organization, even outside a crisis; however, when considering dealing with the trials of a crisis, the message is often difficult to deliver. This complexity results in people giving misinformation, skirting the truth, or just neglecting to address the relevant pieces of information at all. While nonspecific responses may be more comfortable, a lack of clarity will result in more pain in the long term. People will remember what is said and will usually be more displeased if the information is unclear.

Another vital principle of communications is that it is okay for the message to change, obviously within appropriate reason. Indeed, information will inevitably evolve throughout a crisis, and such should be communicated to the relevant audiences as these changes occur. With the available information at a given time, leaders should take a stance and be extremely clear in their messaging. It is critical, especially during a crisis, to tell the truth about the unknowns and address the knowns.

FINANCIAL AND ECONOMIC ISSUES

As we have established, planning does not guarantee that the crisis will not be painful; it helps to increase the chances of coming out intact and ideally more robust. Dealing with the financial impact and economic setbacks that come with most crises will require planning on the front end of the crisis and careful management during the emergency. This section addressed some of the basic financial measures that organizations should develop and implement to effectively weather a crisis.

First, foresight is critical, which means, again, planning financial management strategies before a crisis is imperative. Proper planning can potentially result in reducing losses or diminishing the adverse economic impact on the organization. Next, we discussed the importance of liquidity for an organization to navigate and address the crisis's challenges. Suppose all the organization's assets are locked up in illiquid vehicles. Utilizing them to cover costs or depleted cash flow will likely become even more challenging in a crisis. Further, the lack of liquidity often results in organizations having to pursue alternative strategies to weather the storm, which typically have long-lasting adverse effects on the organization. These alternatives might include furloughing or laying off staff, taking on additional debt (often sparse during a systemic crisis), defaulting on financial obligations (i.e., leases, loans, vendor contracts, etc.), and seeking assistance through bankruptcy.

Insurance is another financial strategy that can be critical and efficient in helping organizations navigating through a crisis. Everything from basic liability insurance to key man (life) insurance and many other types of insurance policies can make the difference whether an organization will make it through a crisis successfully.

OPERATIONAL ISSUES

Similar to the fact that most types of crises will result in some negative financial impact for an organization, the same can be said when it comes to how a situation can negatively affect an organization's operations. There are a variety of ways this can transpire. As previously stated, it is impossible to prepare for every unique scenario considering the broad array of crises that influence operations. However, organizations can focus on developing and communicating several critical action plans for implementation throughout their operational workflows in response to various crises. These strategies could be adjustable as necessary for each circumstance. When it comes to operations and crisis planning, organizations need to create a condensed *playbook* that all employees and providers know well rather than a response plan for every possible scenario or crisis.

A critical operational consideration in planning for and navigating through a crisis is the impact on personnel. Another is maintaining a strong team to continue operations through the crisis event(s). In all personnel matters, the recommendation is to take an objective approach with consistent communication. Physician burnout, union tension, disgruntled employees, and general morale issues can all be considered personnel crises that are detrimental to your business.

Another type of crisis for consideration within operational planning is political and/or regulatory disorder, which can have highly variable effects on different businesses due to multiple factors. Examples include location, patient demographics, payer mix/relationships, and political relationships. For some organizations, politics and operating budgets go hand in hand where local propositions and political matters affect healthcare organizations' funding. A local vote or election could lead to a financial crisis if political differences are not managed effectively. The challenge with these crises or developments is to react without panic and on time. Many leaders want to jump into action or apply the quick bandage when it is often more effective to wait until making a more informed decision to adjust operations adequately. However, the challenge is not to wait too long, realizing that a complete set of information may never be available to feel entirely confident in critical decisions.

Crises of all sorts almost certainly have a detrimental impact on medical groups' and provider organizations' various operations. Since emergencies are typically wide-ranging in possible scenarios and highly unpredictable, it is always challenging to prepare thoroughly for every unique scenario and even more impossible to predict outcomes. Instead, our recommendation is to focus on developing and communicating several essential action plans that can be implemented in response to various crises and adjust those plans as necessary for each circumstance. It is more important to create a condensed playbook that all employees and providers know well than a response plan for every possible scenario or crisis. In some cases, you may implement multiple crisis response plans.

As stated repeatedly, clear communications and proactive preparation are critical to any operational area, all of which become even more important during a crisis. Crises that vary significantly in origin can have similar impacts on operations.

Also, there is often a direct or perhaps indirect correlation between financial challenges and operational issues. Tactics that groups can plan and prepare for financial and operational matters include researching critical information to help navigate a crisis; protecting the vital components of operations impacting financial performance directly; striving to be innovative, dynamic, and flexible throughout a situation; and studying for worst-case scenarios.

PERSONNEL

Closely related to operational challenges, most crises are likely to present issues related to an organization's personnel and human capital. As we saw during the early days and beyond of the COVID-19 crisis, practically all healthcare provider organizations faced some degree of workforce shortages and staffing challenges. This issue included gaps in both clinical and non-clinical or operational personnel. When it comes to personnel challenges during a crisis, the importance of proactive communications can't be overstated: having leaders and mentors, managing people personally and objectively, establishing goals, and creating an organizational culture of respect.

Regarding navigating crises in terms of an organization's people, we have also discussed the importance of leadership during a crisis. Leadership rarely comes from a single person and is also not always exclusive to executive leadership or senior management. We recommend having a crisis management planning team, which may or may not overlap with the actual crisis management team, leading the charge during a real crisis event. Although there should be some overlap, the planning team's primary focus is on just that: planning. This point means there should be plans to mitigate or at least better navigate challenges before the crisis, which absolutely must be centered around the organization's people first. After all, the central nervous system of any healthcare organization is indeed its people.

Organizations must also consider the relevant training and development that their people will need to navigate the challenges that could arise during a crisis. This focal point requires identifying particular needs or critical areas, then designating the leadership and team members to cover these areas. That will help determine the exact training or other development activities that make the most sense.

Likewise, when it comes to personnel with any organization, but especially healthcare services entities, there will always be regulatory requirements and legal considerations for personnel. These will likely undergo amplification and/or modifications during the midst of a crisis, which means it is essential that organizations do not let such things slip through the cracks, despite the chaos that situations can often bring. Staff should feel safe and know that their organization is looking out for their well-being. However, in healthcare, this can be a challenge. During the COVID-19 pandemic, healthcare workers found themselves on the front lines battling the virus daily, which was also associated with the endless responsibility of care continuity and delivery of services to patients. Now consider the operations of providers and hospitals in New Orleans in the wake of the historical floods following Hurricane Katrina. Healthcare workers had to consider their safety and their families, while attempting to help the thousands of people needing care and treatment, and they had to do all of this without consistent power, proper ventilation, and other catastrophic infrastructure issues.

TECHNOLOGY AND CYBERSECURITY CRISIS MANAGEMENT

While the historical and common view of cyber threats is that they are problems for larger organizations that have spent millions fortifying their information technology (IT) infrastructure, this threat is no longer just a vulnerability for such organizations. Indeed, as larger organizations have invested in preventing or combating cyber attacks, this has resulted in medical practices and smaller hospitals becoming the new soft targets for such criminals. Cybersecurity awareness and prevention have been the IT department's worry. Now, the attacks are so debilitating that cybersecurity has become a crisis and a crisis management issue.

Healthcare cybersecurity is a growing concern, as evidenced by the steady rise in hacking and IT security incidents in recent years. Many healthcare organizations have struggled to defend their network perimeter and hold cybercriminals at bay. Now, more than ever, healthcare providers must protect multiple connected medical and non-medical devices. Additionally, there has been an explosion in the number of Internet of Things (IoT) devices integrated into the healthcare industry. Data is the new currency, and cybercriminals will stop at nothing to gain access to this valuable commodity. These offenders are developing more sophisticated methods and techniques to attack healthcare organizations and increase their chances to cash in this data by holding it at ransom or selling it on the black market.

There are significant crisis management implications for cybersecurity that come with operational, financial, and compliance stipulations. For instance, in matters of compliance, the Health Insurance Portability and Accountability Act (HIPAA) security rule requires that healthcare entities covered by HIPAA conduct a security risk analysis (SRA) of their organization. Non-compliance can result in harsh penalties and fines for not complying with these rules.

Regarding cybersecurity and crisis management, we have discussed leadership's importance, specifically from the C-suite down through the organization's ranks. There are also critical considerations related to outside vendors and other third parties. We look at the critical first steps of response when a breach or attack occurs, which starts with disconnecting and even dismantling entire networks and quarantining devices. This act may seem like simply unplugging wires; however, it is much more complicated than that when considering the extensive IT infrastructure and information systems in healthcare organizations. And then, there is navigating the often highly complex web of systems, vendors, networks, and other parties that are connected to in some manner the infected systems.

It is not a question of if an organization will be targeted, but when. Therefore, appropriate plans and procedures must be in place to effectively navigate and successfully resolve crises related to cybersecurity breaches.

POST-CRISIS

Finally, we have looked at the actions that are important for an organization to address after a crisis. We should never go back to business as usual without first reflecting on some of the critical lessons and measuring the impact of a crisis on the organization, its people, and its future. The key to a post-mortem exercise or after-action report is to identify the crucial lessons or takeaways to incorporate in planning for future crises. Both the successes and failures are the best lessons on how an organization can navigate a crisis more effectively, regardless of its nature.

Learning from past experiences is invaluable. We have learned that individuals under pressure will not simply rise to the occasion, but instead will sink to their level of training. The same principle can apply to teams and organizations. The best training will come from lessons learned on the battlefield. But we must not simply observe such lessons; instead, organizations must apply the lessons to planning and preparation for future challenges.

SUMMARY

Healthcare organizations are among the most essential entities during a pandemic. They can also be at the top of the list of those most affected. COVID-19's impact on the industry proved to be no exception, primarily because it was pervasive worldwide. The knowledge attained through the experience and particularly the vulnerabilities exposed have provided invaluable lessons. The purpose of this book is to capture those lessons at many levels and offer an outline and process to follow to prepare for future events, whether they are for local, regional, or intercontinental events.

Master Checklist from the Insurance Institute for Business & Home Safety

1. *Know Your Risks.* Identify the most serious threats to your business by focusing on the disruptions most likely to occur and their impact.

   ✓ *Find and review your county's hazard analysis or mitigation plan, which can be found on the internet.* This will include past threats and disasters in your area and geographical hazards related to severe weather patterns, wildfire concerns, proximity to flood plains, major airports, dams, ports, other companies with hazardous materials, etc.

   ✓ *Consider risks/threats related to your business that stem from the nature of the operation or from specific situations that may originate inside your organization.* Examples include human error, poor training or maintenance, illness, death, theft, fraud, employee morale, the type of equipment used, your IT risks, your building, etc., as well as threats to your community.

   ✓ *Fill out the Know Your Risks form to identify and rank the greatest threats to your business.* (The form is available at https://disastersafety.org/wp-content/uploads/OFB-EZ_Toolkit_IBHS.pdf.)

   ✓ *Develop and document a plan for threats that score the highest (17-25) on the Know Your Risks form.* Assume these threats will strike your business and determine what controls you can implement to minimize your risk.

2. *Know Your Operations.* Understand your business' most critical functions and how to perform them if there is a disruption.

   ✓ *Identify the business functions and processes that are critical to the survival of your business.* Consider: What is your main product/service? What other business functions/processes do you perform to run your overall business such as production/service delivery; manufacturing; customer service; sales/ marketing; purchasing; accounting/finance; human resources; administration; and information technology? What activities do employees perform on a daily, weekly, monthly, and annual basis or other special times of the year?

✓ *Rank these business functions in priority from extremely high to low.* Consider: What are the consequences if the function cannot be performed? Can your business survive without this function? How much downtime can you tolerate for each function?

✓ *Use the Know Your Operations form to document important information for each function.* Start with functions ranked Extremely High and High. Additional functions can wait until your annual update. (The form is available at https://disastersafety. org/wp-content/uploads/OFB-EZ_Toolkit_IBHS.pdf.)

✓ *Consider whether employees need added training to perform functions they do not normally complete but could complete in case of a disruption.*

✓ *Be as specific as possible when documenting procedures for workarounds and/or manual processes.*

3. *Know Your Employees.* Document employee information so you can connect with them before, during, and after a disruption.

✓ *Use the Know Your Employees form to collect contact information for each employee.* This allows you to determine their safety and whereabouts; inform them about the status of operations as well as when, where, and how they should report to work; and provide any added instructions following a disruption. (The form is available at https://disastersafety.org/ wp-content/uploads/OFB-EZ_Toolkit_IBHS.pdf.)

✓ *Note key responsibilities of each employee as well as alternate employees who can perform these tasks.*

✓ *Make sure unique skills are not known by only one person. This may require more employee training.*

✓ *Have employees review and update their contact information at least every six months.*

✓ *Create a Contact Tree so you can quickly call, text, and email employees.* Keep an updated hard copy in case of power or internet outages.

✓ *Designate a phone number and/or intranet site where employees can get status updates and leave messages.*

✓ *Consider technology solutions to simplify the process of reaching your employees.* Low-cost emergency notification systems are available that can reach every employee on every device—instantly, simply, and reliably with one easy click. (However, always maintain a hard copy and manual solutions in case of power/internet outages.)

4. *Know Your Equipment.* Protect critical equipment to keep your business running.

   ✓ *Identify equipment and machinery necessary to perform critical business functions.* If these items failed or were unavailable, the business may have to restrict production of goods and services or be forced to shut down. Examples: a printing press at a print shop or an oven at a bakery. Also consider company-owned vehicles.

   ✓ *Determine how and where you might move these items to safeguard them from a hazardous event when there is advanced warning (such as a hurricane or severe winter weather).* Consider: Can the equipment be easily moved to a safe place in the building or to an alternate location? Can measures be taken to protect the equipment in its current location?

   ✓ *Identify available replacements or alternate options in case equipment becomes damaged or there is a hazardous event without advanced warning.* Consider: Is the equipment customized or one-of-a-kind? How long would it take to reorder? Is the equipment functional or obsolete? If obsolete, how long would it take to replace or get it functional? Are there rental options to temporarily replace the equipment? Can you outsource the end product if equipment cannot be substituted quickly?

   ✓ *Fill out the Know Your Equipment form to document this information.* Use for non-IT equipment only; IT equipment is covered in module 7. (The form is available at https://disastersafety.org/wp-content/uploads/OFB-EZ_Toolkit_IBHS.pdf.) *Save and store photos, purchase invoices, sales receipts, user guides, and warranty information in a dry and safe location.* You should be able to access this information at any time during the event.

5. ***Know How to Reduce Potential Disruptions.*** Identify and plan for potential disruptions so you recover faster.

   ✓ Fill out the Know How to Reduce Potential Disruptions form for information on:
      — Make-up capacities
      — Product and inventory
      — Perishable stock
      — Power
      — Shutdown and start-up plans
      — Miscellaneous

   (The form is available at https://disastersafety.org/wp-content/uploads/OFB-EZ_Toolkit_IBHS.pdf.)

6. ***Know Your Key Customers, Contacts, Suppliers, and Vendors.*** Ensure you can continue service to your customers in case of a disruption.

   ✓ *If possible, avoid relying solely on suppliers and vendors in the same geographic location as your business.*

   ✓ *Establish relationships with alternate or backup suppliers and vendors.*

   ✓ *Request copies of your suppliers' and vendors' business continuity plans.* Your ability to resume operations relies on their ability to deliver to you what you need on time if they experience a disruption.

   ✓ *Fill out the Know Your Key Customers, Contacts, Suppliers, and Vendors form to document contact information.* Key contacts are those you rely on for administration of your business such as accountants, banks, billing/invoicing services, building management or owner, security personnel, insurance agents, internet service providers, payroll providers, public works department, telephone, and utility companies, etc. (The form is available at https://disastersafety.org/wp-content/uploads/OFB-EZ_Toolkit_IBHS.pdf.)

   ✓ *Establish various ways to communicate with customers about the status of your business operations, your product or service, delivery schedules, etc., after a disruption.*

   ✓ *Consider direct telephone calls, a designated telephone number with a recording, text, e-mail, Twitter, Facebook, or announcements on your company website, by radio, or through a newspaper.*

7. *Know Your Information Technology.* Understand your IT needs and develop protection systems.

   ✓ *Develop a severe weather plan to protect equipment.* For example, if severe weather is predicted, shutdown and unplug all computer hardware to avoid damage due to power fluctuations. If flooding may occur, consider elevating or moving equipment offsite. Instruct employees to take laptop computers home each day if you are on weather alert so they can work offsite if necessary.

   ✓ *Determine which data and records are vital to perform the critical functions you found in the Know Your Operations module, and back up this data daily (using servers, desktop PCs/Macs, laptops, or a combination, including operating systems and applications).* It is recommended that data is backed up on one or more types of media. Store a backup copy onsite for use during small disasters, such as a failed hard drive, and store a second copy in a safe offsite location or with a cloud storage provider that can be easily accessed during larger disasters. (The form is available at https://disastersafety.org/wp-content/uploads/OFB-EZ_Toolkit_IBHS.pdf.)

   ✓ *Follow the 3-2-1 backup rule.* You should have three copies of your data. Each copy should be saved to two types of media. And you should keep one backup copy of your data at an offsite location.

   ✓ *Keep a backup copy of your computer's operating system, boot files, critical software, and operations manuals.*

   ✓ *Back up computer files, including payroll, tax, accounting, and production records.*

   ✓ *Maintain an up-to-date copy of computer and Internet login codes and passwords.*

   ✓ *Make arrangements with IT vendors to replace damaged hardware and software, and/or to setup hardware and software at a recovery location.*

   ✓ *Request written estimates for rental or purchase of equipment, shipping costs, and delivery times. Be sure to list these companies on your supplier and vendor form.*

✓ *Keep equipment inventory updated.*

✓ *When flooding is possible, elevate computer equipment stored on the floor.*

✓ *If possible, consult an IT expert to help with the technology needs of your business.*

✓ *Fill out the Know Your Technology form to list the computer equipment, hardware and software, vital records, and your back up processes that you will need to fulfill your critical business functions.* If your computer equipment is damaged or destroyed, you will need to lease or purchase new hardware and replace your software. Make a list of everything you would need to purchase or lease. The important thing is to know what is needed to perform your critical business functions. (The form is available at https://disastersafety.org/wp-content/uploads/OFB-EZ_Toolkit_IBHS.pdf.)

✓ *Establish a maintenance program to keep your IT inventory current and relevant.*

✓ *Review your IT needs and resources every 6 months.*

8. *Know Your Finances.* Ensure your business is financially resilient.

   ✓ *Start an emergency reserve fund.* You may need to purchase supplies or equipment or relocate your business temporarily. Cash during an emergency is recommended, especially in scenarios when the power may go out for prolonged periods forcing business to be conducted on a cash-only basis.

   ✓ *Get a credit card or set up a line of credit.*

   ✓ *Identify financial obligations and expenses that must be paid.* Do not assume that because your area was hit by a disaster that your suppliers, vendors, and creditors are aware of the situation and are granting extensions. Items such as mortgage, lease, or rental payments may still be required.

   ✓ *Consider creating a policy regarding payroll during and after a disaster.* Payroll is often overlooked in business continuity planning. Do not expect employees to continue working without pay during or after a disaster. Be sure employees are aware of your payroll continuity plans so they can plan for their personal financial obligations.

✓ *Have employees sign up for electronic funds transfer (EFT) and arrange for a cloud-based payroll system.*

✓ *Get adequate insurance for your place of business, your contents and inventory, and/or your production processes.* Evaluate your insurance policies and meet regularly with your insurance agent/broker to make sure your coverage is up to date and that you understand what is covered, what is not, deductibles and limits, and how to file a claim. Also discuss the types of insurance coverages available to you such as business owners, business income/business interruption, contingent business income, extra expense insurance, loss of key personnel, and many others.

✓ *Determine if you need separate insurance for flood or earthquake damage (most property insurance policies do not cover these events).*

✓ *Establish clear strategies and procedures for controlling costs, reporting information to appropriate groups, and clearly budgeting so you can track what is spent during a significant disruption.*

✓ *Fill out the Know Your Finances form to develop your financial strategy.* (The form is available at https://disastersafety.org/wp-content/uploads/OFB-EZ_Toolkit_IBHS.pdf.)

✓ *Review your finances every six months.*

9. *Know When to Update and Test Your Plan.* Make sure you are ready any time a disruption could occur.

✓ *Set reminders to review and update your plan every six to twelve months, or any time there are changes to your business.* Consider: Have there been any changes in procedures or business priorities? Have responsibilities changed? Be sure to document this information.

✓ *Use the Know When to Update and Test Your Plan form to test your organization's disaster readiness and learn where you can improve.* (The form is available at https://disastersafety.org/wp-content/uploads/OFB-EZ_Toolkit_IBHS.pdf.)

✓ *Update your plan based on feedback from testing.*

✓ *Keep employees up to date with any plan changes since you will need their help putting the plan into action.*

10. *Know Where to Go for Help.* Build ties with your community and outside agencies who can help you recover quickly from a disaster.

✓ *Get to know community leaders, emergency management office staff (from police and fire departments and emergency medical services), and other key staff from government agencies, utility companies, etc., who can provide helpful information during a disaster.*

✓ *Use the Know Where to Go for Help form to gather information from helpful resources.* (The form is available at https://disastersafety.org/wp-content/uploads/OFB-EZ_Toolkit_IBHS.pdf.)

Note: OFB-EZ™ is a program of the Insurance Institute for Business & Home Safety. Download this document at disastersafety.org/ofb-ez

Source: Insurance Institute for Business & Home Safety. https://disastersafety.org/wp-content/uploads/2020/09/ofb-ez_Master-Checklist.pdf. Accessed April 16, 2021.

CPSIA information can be obtained
at www.ICGtesting.com
Printed in the USA
BVHW091912190921
617038BV00003B/11